CHARACTERS

A one-year exploration of the Bible
through the lives of its people.

VOLUME SIX

The Followers

LifeWay Press® • Nashville, Tennessee

EDITORIAL TEAM

Brandon Hiltibidal
Director, Discipleship and Groups Ministry

Brian Daniel
Manager, Short-Term Discipleship

Joel Polk
Editorial Team Leader

Michael Kelley
Content Developer

David Briscoe
Content Developer

G.B. Howell Jr.
Content Developer

Rob Tims
Content Editor

Laura Magness
Content Editor

Gena Rogers
Production Editor

Darin Clark
Art Director

Denise Wells
Designer

Lauren Rives
Designer

From the creators of *Explore the Bible, Explore the Bible: Characters* is a seven-volume resource that examines the lives of biblical characters within the historical, cultural, and biblical context of Scripture. Each six-session volume includes videos to help your group understand the way each character fits into the storyline of the Bible.

© 2020 LifeWay Press®

ISBN 978-1-4300-7040-5 • Item 005823508
Dewey decimal classification: 220.92
Subject headings: BIBLE. N.T.--BIOGRAPHY / APOSTLES

We believe that the Bible has God for its author; salvation for its end; and truth, without any mixture of error, for its matter and that all Scripture is totally true and trustworthy. To review LifeWay's doctrinal guideline, please visit lifeway.com/doctrinalguideline.

Unless otherwise noted, Scripture quotations are taken from the Christian Standard Bible®, Copyright © 2017 by Holman Bible Publishers. Used by permission. Christian Standard Bible® and CSB® are federally registered trademarks of Holman Bible Publishers. Scripture quotations marked (ESV) are from the ESV® Bible (The Holy Bible, English Standard Version®), copyright © 2001 by Crossway, a publishing ministry of Good News Publishers. Used by permission. All rights reserved. Scripture quotations marked (NIV) are taken from the Holy Bible, New International Version®, NIV®. Copyright © 1973, 1978, 1984, 2011 by Biblica, Inc.™ Used by permission of Zondervan. All rights reserved worldwide. www.zondervan.com. The "NIV" and "New International Version" are trademarks registered in the United States Patent and Trademark Office by Biblica, Inc.™ Scripture quotations marked (NASB) are taken from the New American Standard Bible® (NASB), Copyright © 1960, 1962, 1963, 1968, 1971, 1972, 1973, 1975, 1977, 1995 by The Lockman Foundation. Used by permission. www.lockman.org.

To order additional copies of this resource, write to LifeWay Resources Customer Service; One LifeWay Plaza; Nashville, TN 37234; fax 615-251-5933; call toll free 800-458-2772; or order online at LifeWay. com; email orderentry@lifeway.com.

Printed in the United States of America

Groups Ministry Publishing • LifeWay Resources • One LifeWay Plaza • Nashville, TN 37234

CONTENTS

ABOUT EXPLORE THE BIBLE

The Whole Truth, Book by Book

Explore the Bible is an ongoing family of Bible study resources that guides the whole church through the only source of the truth on which we can rely: God's Word. Each session frames Scripture with biblical and historical context vital to understanding its original intent, and unpacks the transforming truth of God's Word in a manner that is practical, age-appropriate, and repeatable over a lifetime.

Find out more at goExploreTheBible.com.

HOW TO USE THIS STUDY

This Bible study includes six sessions of content for group and personal study. Regardless of what day of the week your group meets, each session begins with group study. Each group session utilizes the following elements to facilitate simple yet meaningful interaction among group members and with God's Word.

INTRODUCTION

This page includes introductory content and questions to get the conversation started each time your group meets.

GROUP DISCUSSION

Each session has a corresponding teaching video to introduce the story. These videos have been created specifically to teach the group more about the biblical figure being studied. After watching the video, continue the group discussion by reading the Scripture passages and discussing the questions that follow. Finally, conclude each group session with a time of prayer, reflecting on what you discussed.

BIOGRAPHY AND FURTHER INSIGHT MOMENT

These sections provide more in-depth information regarding the biblical character being spotlighted each session and can be included in the group discussion or personal study times.

PERSONAL STUDY

Three personal studies are provided for each session to take individuals deeper into Scripture and to supplement the content introduced in the group study. With biblical teaching and introspective questions, these sections challenge individuals to grow in their understanding of God's Word and to respond in faith.

LEADER GUIDE

A tear out leader guide for each session is provided on pages 95-106. This section also includes sample answers or discussion prompts to help you jump start or steer the conversation.

VOLUME SIX

The Followers

PHILIP

A Growing Follower

INTRODUCTION

What does it mean to be spiritually mature? It is easy to identify someone who is physically mature and possibly emotionally mature, but how do you know if someone is spiritually mature?

Spiritual maturity results from a full knowledge of the biblical teaching about Jesus and salvation and from correct application of this teaching to everyday life. One can say that she is a mature Christian to the degree that she knows and lives by biblical truth. When we come to know Jesus as our Savior, we are "babes in Christ." We drink spiritual milk and learn spiritual basics, but we are expected to move on to more solid spiritual food in time. Maturity is a natural part of our spiritual lives. If we aren't growing, something is wrong.

While the bulk of the Bible's dealing with this concept takes place in the New Testament Epistles, throughout the Bible are examples of people maturing in their faith as they progress in their age and in their walk with the Lord. Philip is one such person.

Philip, one of Jesus' disciples, showed signs of consistent growth over the course of his life. Philip "grew up" in Jesus and changed for the better. At first, Philip's understanding of who Jesus was lacked clarity and insight into Jesus' true self. As Philip spent three years with Jesus and his fellow apostles, Philip's maturity grew.

How have you changed for the better over the years?

What has caused you to grow most in your faith in Jesus?

Watch the video teaching for Session 1 to discover "The World of Philip," then continue the group discussion.

FOCUS ATTENTION

When was the last time you got so excited about something that you couldn't wait to tell others? What was it, and how did you go about sharing your news?

EXPLORE THE TEXT

As a group, read John 1:43-46.

When you look at Philip's story here, what example is there for us to follow?

As a group, read John 6:1-7.

In another story about Philip's journey with Jesus, the Lord tested him when a crisis arose. How would you describe Philip in this encounter with Jesus?

As a group, read John 12:20-32.

What is significant about Philip, the Greeks who approached Jesus, and the timing of Jesus' reply to the request for an audience with Him?

As a group, read John 14:8-14.

How would you describe Jesus' response to Philip's request to show him and his fellow apostles the Father?

As a group, read Acts 8:4-8,26-40.

What can we know about Philip in this post-resurrection account of his ministry as an apostle? How is he different than he was in the previous passages?

APPLY THE TEXT

We may also mirror the journey that Philip took with Jesus. Our understanding of who Jesus is may have deepened over the years as we spend time worshiping Him, studying His Word, and serving Him. Philip came to understand and believe that Jesus was God's resurrected Son, in whom salvation is found. This turned Philip into a teacher and evangelist who was not shy about telling others about Jesus.

With which part of Philip's life can you most easily identify? His early days or his time after Jesus' resurrection? Explain.

For a time, Philip had misunderstandings about who Jesus was. Is there any aspect of Jesus' life and ministry that is confusing to you?

Who do you know who needs to hear the good news about Jesus and the reality that they can be forgiven of their sin and have a new life in Christ? What would it take for you to have the boldness of Philip and share the good news with them this week?

Close your group time in prayer, reflecting on what you have discussed.

PHILIP

KEY VERSE

Philip found Nathanael and told him, "We have found the one Moses wrote about in the law (and so did the prophets): Jesus the son of Joseph, from Nazareth."

— John 1:45

BASIC FACTS

1. One of Jesus' early followers; a resident of Bethsaida in Galilee, the hometown also of Simon Peter and Andrew.

2. Name *Philip* is Greek; means "lover of horses."

3. No family information given in Scripture; not to be confused with Philip the deacon and evangelist in Acts (Acts 6:5; 8:4-40; 21:8-9).

4. Was well-versed in Old Testament regarding the promised Messiah; may have been a disciple of John the Baptist until Jesus called him.

5. Named an apostle by Jesus and continued as a church leader after Jesus' resurrection and ascension.

6. No information in Scripture concerning his death.

TIMELINE

AD 30–40

- Jesus' ministry, crucifixion, resurrection, ascension 30–33
- Philip follows Jesus; becomes an apostle 30
- Birth of the church during Pentecost 33
- Stephen's martyrdom 33
- Conversion of Saul (Paul) 33

AD 40–50

- Herod Agrippa I rules in Judea 41–44
- Barnabas brings Paul to Antioch 43
- Paul's first missionary journey 47–48
- Jerusalem Council 49
- Claudius expels Jews from Rome 49

KNOWN FOR

1. Philip is identified only as being among the twelve apostles in the three Synoptic Gospels and Acts (Matt. 10:3; Mark 3:18; Luke 6:14; Acts 1:13). Only John's Gospel provides several longer accounts of Philip's activities.

2. Jesus intentionally found Philip and called him to follow as a disciple. Philip responded by immediately inviting his friend Nathanael (also known as Bartholomew) to "come and see" Jesus the Messiah (John 1:43-46).

3. Jesus put Philip's faith in God to the test by challenging Philip to propose how they could provide food for five thousand people who had been listening to Jesus teach (John 6:5-6).

4. At a Passover festival in Jerusalem, some Greek-speaking worshipers asked Philip to facilitate their meeting Jesus. Philip and Andrew told Jesus of the request, prompting Him to declare that His time of suffering and sacrifice had come (John 12:20-23).

5. Although not identified individually by name, Philip presumably was present at the first Lord's Supper, in the garden when Jesus was arrested, and with the other disciples on occasions when the risen Christ appeared to the group, commissioned them, and then ascended.

AD 50-60

- Paul's second missionary journey 50–52
- Paul's third missionary journey 53–57
- Antonius Felix governor of Judea 52–60
- Synoptic Gospels written 55–59
- Paul arrested in Jerusalem; sent to Rome 57–59

AD 60-70

- Paul under house arrest in Rome 61–62
- Apostle James martyred In Jerusalem 62
- Great fire in Rome 64
- Apostle Peter martyred in Rome 66
- Apostle Paul martyred in Rome 67

To Be a Disciple

By William B. Tolar

The New Testament uses the Greek word *mathetai* on many occasions to include any and all people who profess faith in Jesus as the Messiah and who seek to follow His teachings. On other occasions, though, the word designates that inner group of especially called and commissioned followers, also called "apostles" or "the Twelve." Paul later used the Greek word for *apostle* to signify a few persons who were not in the original Twelve. All the apostles were disciples, but not all disciples were apostles. Therefore, some ambiguity and lack of precision are in the use of both "disciple" and "apostle." The context of the word within its particular passage is key to interpreting its meaning.

Disciple was Jesus' favorite word to designate His followers, and the most widely used word in the New Testament for them. The Greek word translated *disciple* occurs a total of 261 times, and all but about 30 (which occur in Acts) are in the four Gospels. Paul never used "disciple." The Gospel writers (and Jesus) never used the Greek word translated *Christian* to designate a follower of Jesus. That word occurs only three times in our New Testament (see Acts 11:26; 26:28; 1 Peter 4:16).

In Matthew 19:16-30, a man came to Jesus and asked what he had to do to have eternal life. When Jesus told him to go and sell everything, give it to the poor, then follow Him, the man did not follow Christ. He did not become a "disciple." Jesus used the occasion to teach His "disciples" (v. 23) how spiritually dangerous material possessions are and how hard it is not to let wealth be an idol that usurps God's place.

When the disciples (probably the twelve apostles) responded with amazement, Jesus reminded them that all things are possible with God—even the converting of the wealthy. Jesus did not command every disciple to sell everything and give it away, for obviously some of the women followers (according to the Gospels) had wealth and used it to support Jesus' ministry. All true disciples, though, had to be willing—they had to have the attitude of complete obedience and total sacrifice if they were to be His disciples. This is still true today.

Jesus' expectations of His disciples were much higher than those of other religious leaders of His day. Jesus demanded a total commitment and allegiance to Him as the Son of God and Messiah that other teachers did not make of their disciples. When Peter responded by declaring that he and the others (probably meaning the Twelve) had "left everything and followed" Him, Jesus replied with an astounding promise (see Matt. 19:27-29). They would in the future "sit on twelve thrones, judging the twelve tribes of Israel." Whatever price they had paid would be rewarded with "a hundred times more" as well as with "eternal life." No other teacher could offer his disciples such a future.

William B. Tolar, "To Be a Disciple," *Biblical Illustrator*, Fall 2004.

Looking at the Sea of Galilee in the distance, as seen from the porch of the Church of the Beatitudes, the traditional site of Jesus' first sermon.

Illustrator Photo/ Bob Schatz (19/7/10)

Read John 1:43-46.

In this short narrative, Jesus found Philip (v. 43). Philip in turn found Nathanael and reported to Nathanael, "We have found" Him (v. 45). This theme of "finding" was introduced in the previous section of Scripture (see 1:41) in connection with "following" and with the confession by Andrew that Jesus was the Messiah. But it is intriguing to ask the very simple question concerning these stories: Who really finds whom? Christians have frequently been known to say that they "found" Christ or "found" faith as Andrew and Philip reported, but maybe Jesus' perspective in these stories could profitably alter such a self-centered view of salvation. It was not Jesus who was lost!

In this part of John's gospel, the finding process leads Philip to make another important confession. The translation "the one Moses wrote about in the Law, and about whom the prophets also wrote" (v. 45, NIV) seems to catch the point of the text pretty well. What is meant is that Scripture bears witness to Jesus, a theme that is repeated elsewhere in this Gospel (see 5:39-40; 19:36; Luke 24:27).

What are some stories from the Old Testament that point to Jesus as the coming Messiah?

The companion confession concerning Jesus of Nazareth, the son of Joseph (1:45), forms a magnificent bridge to the next confession by Nathanael, that is, that Jesus was the "Son of God" (1:49). But one of the great themes in this Gospel is the theme of misunderstanding. People constantly think they know who Jesus is, and they think they know the answer to His origin. Their perceptions are actually skewed, and therefore their conclusions usually need major revision.

What motivates a person to follow Jesus? How much does a person need to know to follow Him?

Philip was introduced in this story as being from Bethsaida, the home city of Andrew and Peter. Although Bethsaida was technically located in the region of Gaulanitis, just outside the borders of Herod's jurisdiction of Galilee, in popular thinking it seems to have been included in the land around Galilee, particularly after the beginning of the Jewish War.

Philip thought that Jesus was the person the Old Testament pointed to as the Messiah. How might you respond to someone who views Jesus as just a teacher or just a good person?

Have you grown closer to Jesus over the years? Explain.

Read John 6:1-9.

Jesus, Philip, and the disciples went to the other side of the sea. The area where the feeding occurred would likely be the more barren hillsides east of the lake, directly across from Tiberias, and not the traditional site visited by pilgrims at Tabgha on the northwest shore. The crowds that followed Jesus to this area were impressed by the signs He performed on the sick, and they were willing to follow Him even into remote areas. The hills in this region would provide an ideal place for Jesus to climb and sit down with His disciples (see v. 3). It was here that Jesus would pose a question to Philip that would reveal his thinking as well as the fact he still had much to learn about Jesus.

We all have much to learn about Jesus. What is the most important or meaningful thing you have learned about Him in the last year?

Jesus frequently chose a mountain setting for His ministry, perhaps because mountains were regarded as a crucial symbolic place of divine encounter (see Matt 4:8; 14:23; 17:1; 21:1; 28:16). Moreover, sitting was a symbol of authority (see Matt 23:2; 25:31).

The history of Israel was mountain oriented from the near sacrifice of Isaac at Moriah, to the call of Moses and the giving of the law at Sinai, to the place chosen for the temple on Mount Moriah, and the trial of Yahweh with Elijah at Mount Carmel. The people of Israel knew the importance of mountain experiences. Their God was a high and exalted God (Isa. 6:1). To come to the God of the mountain was therefore to come with fear and expectation. It is also significant to remember that in the minds of the Jews, one always went up to Jerusalem, not merely in the geographical sense. These truths would have been known by Philip, whom Jesus was about to single out and ask a probing question to discover just how much he understood about the real Jesus.

Mountains were important to the Jewish people. They tended to be places where they met with God. Where have you most recently felt like you have met with God?

The time of this story was Passover, the strategic historical time when God saved His people from slavery in Egypt. But Passover for John was also the time when God had provided the ultimate rescue through the Savior of the world (see John 4:42). The comparison with Moses was clearly intended as John brought together a number of themes in this chapter.

The feeding of the five thousand is the only miracle that appears in all four Gospels. The feeding story in this Gospel is initiated with a probing question concerning resources for food. According to Mark 6:35-37, it was the disciples who raised the issue of the crowd being fed, to which Jesus replied, "You give them something to eat" (6:37).

John only records Jesus' question to Philip: "Where shall we buy bread?" In this story the evangelist, John, made sure he interpreted Jesus' question for the reader. It was not a question for information, but a question to probe whether or not Philip understood who Jesus was (John 6:6).

Philip's answer proved the point. Rather than focusing on Jesus, Philip's mental computer began to work like a cash register, and all he could think about was the cost of just a little bread for each person. It was fast approaching the better part of a year's wages (see John 6:7). To be fair to Philip, Jesus' question was a leading one, and Philip's mind followed the easy path. But the answer was not what Jesus sought. For Philip, however, the answer was hopelessness.

Andrew, the helper, tried to solve the problem in another way. He began immediately to search for picnic resources in that barren place, but his search also ended in failure, according to his thinking. All he found was a boy in the crowd who had a lunch with barley loaves (the bread of the poor) and two fish (John 6:9). Andrew's answer was also hopelessness.

When have you felt hopeless? What emotions did you encounter during that time?

Read Acts 8:26-40.

The southernmost of the five chief Philistine cities, Gaza, lay about fifty miles southwest of Jerusalem. It was destroyed about 98 BC and later rebuilt by Pompey. Philip, sent by an angel to that region, would soon enter a new phase of ministry. Surely the place and timing seemed inappropriate. Why would God move him from an area-wide evangelistic campaign just getting underway in Samaria, down to this lonely desert road? Luke wants us to see what the early Christians were really like. Contrast Philip with Jonah. Empowered by the Holy Spirit, this lay evangelist went wherever God sent. Philip was on his way to the end of the Palestinian world of that time. South and west of Gaza the desert trailed off across Sinai into Egypt. There was nothing.

Philip was in God's plan again and functioning through the Spirit. Gaza was not the target at all, but rather an Ethiopian eunuch, treasurer to the queen, on his way home from temple worship, presumably in an ox-drawn chariot.

Have you ever felt that someone you encountered in your day-to-day activities was a "divine appointment" (someone whose path God crossed with yours so you could talk about Jesus)? What happened?

How easy we find it to picture Philip plodding southward on that desert road, casually observing the common sight of a foreign visitor returning from Jerusalem and, in the custom of the day, reading aloud, this time from Isaiah 53. What might the evangelist have been thinking? Perhaps mixed emotions—the loneliness of the place, possibly regret at leaving the thriving effort in Samaria, even a wish that this stranger could really understand the Messiah of whom the prophet had written. Since an ox-drawn vehicle hardly moved at blazing speed, the Spirit could easily say to Philip, "Catch that chariot!"

Philip's question, "Do you understand what you're reading?" no doubt placed in his mind by the Holy Spirit, illustrates a basic theme in Luke and Acts—how to find Jesus in the Old Testament. Luke had already written to Theophilus that Jesus is the key to understanding that ancient Scripture (see Luke 24:45).

This problem has never disappeared. People caught up in religion of various kinds not only fail to understand the intricacies of their chosen religion, but make no connection between that dogma and God's genuine revelation through the Bible. Has there ever been a better invitation to proclaim the gospel than this? The official invited Philip to come up and sit with him.

If you had the opportunity to share Jesus with a stranger, where would you begin?

Imagine the exhilaration in Philip's heart as he realized why the Spirit had sent him to the desert. Here is a good man in need of grace, a serious searcher whose religion had not satisfied his quest for reality. God had prepared not only his heart, but his mind. What better Old Testament text from which to preach Jesus than Isaiah 53:7-8.

Jesus had said repeatedly he had not come to wrest power from the Romans and build an earthly kingdom. "The Son of Man did not come to be served but to serve" (Mark 10:45) and even to die. This Christian interpretation of Isaiah Philip knew well. He was quite prepared to explain Jesus from this text.

Not only did the eunuch invite Philip to sit with him and explain the text, but he asked the very questions that would lead to an introduction of the Savior. Could Philip have begun somewhere in Deuteronomy or Job and explained the new covenant gospel to this man? Quite probably. But God made it much easier. With joy Philip explained, and with joy Luke recorded this good man hearing for the first time the good news about Jesus.

Who is the first person to tell you about the good news of Jesus? Where were you, and what were the circumstances?

NICODEMUS
A Curious Follower

INTRODUCTION

Have you ever wished that you could start life all over again?

At one time or another, we have all had regrets. But starting over in our physical life will not solve our problems. Our real need is to be born again spiritually. This is why Jesus told the teacher Nicodemus, "You must be born again" (John 3:7). The birth that Jesus spoke of was a new heavenly birth, one that only the Holy Spirit can bring about.

The believer possesses a new life from God through the process of spiritual birth. Christians are born of God (John 1:12-13), and only through this spiritual birth can one participate in the kingdom of God and receive His Spirit. Those born into God's family reflect His righteous character, and they are freed from habitual sin.

The initial experience of being born again is followed by a continuing renewal in the life of the Christian. The newborn are to desire the pure milk of God's Word in order to grow (1 Pet. 2:2). Paul encourages an ongoing transformation in all believers by commanding us to renew our thoughts and attitudes (Rom. 12:2; Eph. 4:23).

Contrary to what many people think, the Christian life is not boring, stagnant, or uneventful. The believer's inner self is renewed daily (2 Cor. 4:16), and all of us are constantly in the process of becoming the men and women God wants us to be (Col. 3:10). The Lord wants us to become more like Him every day.

Why is change so difficult for most people?

What is one change in your life you embraced with a positive attitude?

*Watch the video teaching for Session 2 to discover "The World of Nicodemus,"
then continue the group discussion.*

FOCUS ATTENTION

When you think about change, who do you know who has changed in positive ways over the time you've known him or her? What factors cause people to take action and change some aspect of themselves or their lives?

EXPLORE THE TEXT

As a group, read John 3:1-3.

What do we learn about Nicodemus in these verses? What was missing in his life, according to Jesus (v. 3)?

As a group, read John 3:4-8.

What did Jesus want Nicodemus to know by His statement in verse 8? How does this apply to us?

As a group, read John 3:9-13.

What did Nicodemus mean by his question in verse 9? What can we learn from Jesus' response to him?

As a group, read John 3:14-16.

What does the reference to Moses and the snake being lifted up have to do with John 3:16?

As a group, read John 3:17-18.

Why might some people struggle with the teachings in these verses?

As a group, read John 3:19-21.

In light of Jesus' earlier conversation with Nicodemus, why do you believe Jesus ended His interaction with "Israel's teacher" in this way?

APPLY THE TEXT

Jesus clearly explained the truth to Nicodemus, the truth that to be a member of God's spiritual family, a person must experience a second birth. This second birth is not a physical one, but rather a spiritual one in which a person places faith and trust in Jesus alone.

Why do people find it difficult to accept Jesus' testimony about how one comes into His eternal family?

How can we help others accept Jesus' offer of forgiveness?

How does the growing idea that truth is relative and even geographical make it harder for people to accept God's Word and salvation through Christ?

Close your group time in prayer, reflecting on what you have discussed.

NICODEMUS

KEY VERSE

This man came to him at night and said, "Rabbi, we know that you are a teacher who has come from God, for no one could perform these signs you do unless God were with him."

— John 3:2

BASIC FACTS

1. Jewish ruling elder who became a secret disciple after hearing Jesus explain the need to be born again by the Spirit.

2. Name *Nicodemus* is of Greek origin, meaning "victor of (or over) the people"; a similar Hebrew name possibly means "innocent of blood."

3. No family information about Nicodemus appears in Scripture.

4. Member of the Pharisees, the Jewish religious sect known for strict adherence to Mosaic law and traditions.

TIMELINE

AD 30–40	AD 40–50
Jesus' ministry, crucifixion, resurrection, ascension 30–33	Herod Agrippa I rules in Judea 41–44
Nicodemus approaches Jesus by night 31	Barnabas brings Paul to Antioch 43
Birth of the church during Pentecost 33	Paul's first missionary journey 47–48
Stephen's martyrdom 33	Jerusalem Council 49
Conversion of Saul (Paul) 33	Claudius expels Jews from Rome 49

KNOWN FOR

1. Accounts of Nicodemus's activities are found in Scripture only in John's Gospel.

2. Nicodemus went to meet Jesus at night to say that he respected Jesus as a teacher who had come from God. Jesus explained to Nicodemus that people must be born again by the Spirit to enter God's kingdom (John 3:1-8).

3. Nicodemus heard Jesus speak perhaps the most memorable verse in the New Testament, John 3:16.

4. Nicodemus dared to defend Jesus before his fellow Pharisees who had increasingly determined to reject Jesus' claims as the Messiah.

5. Nicodemus assisted Joseph of Arimathea in removing Jesus' body from the cross, preparing the body for burial, and laying Jesus' body in a new tomb near the crucifixion site (John 19:38-42).

AD 50-60

- Paul's second missionary journey 50–52
- Paul's third missionary journey 53–57
- Antonius Felix governor of Judea 52–60
- Synoptic Gospels written 55–59
- Paul arrested in Jerusalem; sent to Rome 57–59

AD 60-70

- Paul under house arrest in Rome 61–62
- Apostle James martyred In Jerusalem 62
- Great fire in Rome 64
- Apostle Peter martyred in Rome 66
- Apostle Paul martyred in Rome 67

A Man Named Nicodemus

By Randall L. Adkisson

Nicodemus is a pivotal character in the Gospel of John. Yet apart from the three appearances in the fourth Gospel (chs. 3, 7, and 19), we know little about his life. Neither Matthew, Mark, nor Luke referred to Nicodemus.

The Biblical Information

In the first century, the Pharisees were one of the prominent religious and political parties of Israel. As a Pharisee, Nicodemus enjoyed prominence and respect.

The Pharisees believed in a resurrection from the dead. They maintained a strict adherence to the law of Moses. Along with the written law, the Pharisees held strongly to the "oral law" or the interpretations of the law by Pharisaic scholars. In general, Pharisees belonged to the common class of society. Many were tradesmen, merchants, or shopkeepers.

Designated a "ruler of the Jews," Nicodemus was a member of the Sanhedrin. The Sanhedrin was the chief ruling council of Israel, consisting of seventy-one elders. Although under the imperial rule of the Romans, the Sanhedrin exercised considerable authority in both religious and governmental affairs.

Jesus addressed Nicodemus as "the teacher of Israel" (ESV). Perhaps this means that Nicodemus was a scribe, one especially trained in the interpretation of the Scripture and the law. He was thus a respected and influential teacher.

Scripture also tells us Nicodemus provided one hundred pounds of myrrh and aloes to prepare for Jesus' burial. The gift's great expense may indicate that Nicodemus was wealthy.

Importance to the Fourth Gospel

Nicodemus would be important to our understanding and faith if he appeared only in John 3. Jesus' dialogue with Nicodemus emphasized the essence of the New Testament message of judgment and grace. Coming as it does at the beginning of John's Gospel, it

Exterior courtyard at the Church of the Holy Sepulcher in Jerusalem. Hadrian, early in the 2nd cent. AD, desecrated the site by building a temple to Aphrodite there. Constantine later destroyed the Hadrian temple and dedicated the site in 335 in the name of Christianity. Archaeologists have long accepted this as the traditional site of Jesus' crucifixion and burial.

Illustrator Photo/ James Mclemore (13/26/6)

foreshadows the themes of darkness and light, attesting signs, the kingdom, the Spirit, witness, incarnation, the cross, belief, judgment, and salvation.

The Gospel reveals the importance of Nicodemus's position on the Sanhedrin when he was the only one to rise to Jesus' defense. When Nicodemus said, "Our law doesn't judge a man before it hears from him" (John 7:51), the Gospel reader knows that Nicodemus has taken the time to do just that.

The last appearance of Nicodemus pairs him with Joseph of Arimathea, a secret disciple (19:38). At Jesus' death, Joseph overcame his fear of having too close an association with Jesus and requested of Pilate the privilege of taking Jesus' body for burial. Nicodemus, too, overcame his reticence of association and joined Joseph, contributing costly spices for preparing Jesus' body for burial. John reported this was the Nicodemus who previously came to Jesus by night (see 7:50; 19:39). With such a public and official display of devotion, neither Joseph nor Nicodemus could expect to remain a secret disciple. With his meticulous reporting of Nicodemus's past encounters with Jesus, John wanted the Gospel reader to identify in this Pharisaic teacher a gradual but clear movement toward open belief.

Randall L. Adkisson, "A Man Named Nicodemus," *Biblical Illustrator,* Winter 2006-07.

Read John 3:1-8,16-21.

A relationship with God doesn't begin with adjusting our circumstances or behaviors. It begins with a heart changed by Jesus by grace through faith. We can often forget the dramatic change that our coming to faith brought. After all, we were not bad people who needed to be made good. We were dead and had to be brought to life. We are eternally changed because of what God did for us. Christ's sacrifice means that we can join in a restored relationship with Him, now and forever.

What do we learn about Nicodemus in these verses? What might have drawn Him to Jesus?

Nicodemus was a Pharisee and a ruler of the Jews, meaning he was a member of the Sanhedrin—the supreme judicial council in Jewish life. From these facts we can assume that he was likely rich, highly educated, interested in spiritual matters, and knowledgeable about Old Testament Scripture. And yet, some longing or unrest caused this theologian to approach a humble carpenter, graciously acknowledging Jesus as a teacher from God, forming a relationship that would change his life forever.

To be "born again" means to experience a birth from above. Jesus is referencing salvation—the Holy Spirit's work in the life of an individual to bring a person into the family of God. Before we are born again, we may suspect that something isn't right and that our lives need to change, but we will not understand why until we address the true source—our relationship, or lack thereof, with Christ.

How have you seen sin distort and twist people's identities, including your own? What was the state of your relationship with Christ in those times?

Without God's grace, we are spiritually hopeless. But from the beginning of creation, God had a plan to save us by His great grace. When we realize our need for His grace, our relationship with God becomes the defining element of our lives.

God's love provided salvation for the world through the gift and sacrifice of His Son, but salvation comes only to those who believe in Christ (3:18). When we believe in Him, we are restored to a right relationship with God.

What impact do God's mercy, love, and grace have on your relationship with Him? What impact can it have on your relationship with others?

God's mercy, love, and grace bring about change. Mercy is the disposition to act compassionately in response to the plight of others in need. Grace describes God's undeserved favor toward all who have sinned against Him. Paul described the timing of Christ's death as "while we were still helpless, at the right time" (Rom. 5:6). Christ did not die for us when we were worthy of being saved; He died when we were at our absolute worst—broken and hopeless.

What does it mean to "believe" in Jesus? Take a minute to read James 2:19. What kind of action does this believing require?

Read John 3:4-18.

The text doesn't tell us Nicodemus's motive for coming to Jesus. When Nicodemus called Jesus "Rabbi," he (a member of the Jewish ruling council) placed himself in the role of student. The conversation that unfolded led him to eternal life with God.

Why do you think Nicodemus traveled to meet Jesus at nighttime?

If we view these first fifteen verses of chapter 3 as a series of questions and answers, the first question might look like this: "Are you here to bring in the kingdom?" And Jesus' first answer is, "You will never see the kingdom without being born again." Jesus got right to the heart of the problem. He told the teacher he must be "born again." Unless God changes our hearts His way, from the inside out, any discussion of the kingdom is useless.

Now the second question surfaces: "How can a man be born when he is old?" The answer must have hit Nicodemus right between the eyes: "No one can enter the kingdom of God unless he is born of water and the Spirit." Verse 3 deals with the way of the new birth, and verse 5 talks about the process. Being "born of the Spirit" means the change provided at the time of faith in Christ.

In this fascinating conversation, Jesus moves from the metaphor of birth to that of a breeze. Human effort can only produce human results (see John 1:13), but the "pneuma"—the Spirit—is a different story. This is a spiritual mystery known only to God and difficult to explain in terms humans can grasp. God brings the breeze when and where He chooses. Life change comes from the presence of the Holy Spirit.

Why are we so convinced that we have to earn a place in God's heaven? Why is the concept of "free" so difficult for some people to accept when it comes to God's offer of forgiveness in Christ?

Eternal life comes not because of anything we do. Salvation comes as a free gift when we believe what God has said: "Whoever believes in Him shall not perish but have eternal life." Four times in two verses (vv. 16,18) Jesus uses variations of the word *believe*. Jesus classified the entire human race into two groups—those who believe and are not condemned, and those who do not believe and are condemned already. The gospel begins with God's love, continues through the cross and the empty tomb, and results in eternal life for those who believe. Those who refuse God's gift are alienated from Him without hope for both the present and the future.

Did all this happen for judgment and condemnation? No. That was never God's purpose. Notice how central Jesus is to the passage. Verse 17 talks about God's saving the world through Him. Every human being has a choice—eternal life or eternal death. And as the Bible describes it, to perish is not to cease to exist, but to experience utter failure, futility, and loss—an eternity without God.

If you were Nicodemus, what thoughts and emotions might you have while Jesus is correcting your understanding of what it takes to be in God's presence when you die?

Now we see the verdict. People reject Christ because of evil deeds and because they hate the light. God does not label their deeds evil because they love darkness; they love darkness because that is their very nature. What possible excuses keep people from Christ? This passage tells us they refuse light because it shows up the darkness in their own lives. Believers live in the light, while unbelievers live in the darkness. Those who practice the truth, who continuously live in the light of God's Spirit, demonstrate that their righteousness—the right standing we have before God once our sins are forgiven—has been brought about by God.

Read John 3:3-5.

The Jews had two ways in which they used repetition for emphasis, and Jesus used them both in His conversation with Nicodemus. You can see such an emphasis in the Old Testament Book of Isaiah. In chapter 6, the seraphim in the heavenly throne room of God are depicted singing "Holy, holy, holy" in antiphonal response. When you see the repetition of a word in Scripture, you are witnessing a technique used throughout the Bible. When the Jews wanted to make something emphatic, instead of adding an exclamation point or using italics, they would simply repeat it. Jesus did this in His conversation with the Jewish leader Nicodemus.

When you communicate something really important, how do you do it?

When Jesus introduced His necessary condition, He didn't simply say, "Unless one is born again, he cannot see the kingdom of God." Instead, He began by saying, "Truly, truly," which in the original language would have read, "amēn, amēn." From time to time, Jesus prefaced His teaching by the repetition of the word "amen," and this is one of those occasions. When He wanted to say, "Here's something that's very important," He would say, "Truly, truly."

If you hear someone say that it is not necessary to be born again in order to enter the kingdom of heaven, remember that was not what Jesus said. When you feel conflicted about whether being born again is or is not a requirement, you will have to decide who speaks with the supreme authority for the Christian church. The Lord of the church says, with emphasis, "Truly, truly, I say to you, unless one is born again, he cannot see the kingdom of God."

Where are you in the spiritual birthing process? Would you say you are:
(1) not yet conceived (2) developing, but not born (3) a "babe in Christ"
(4) a maturing, growing disciple?

The Jews used repetition in a second way. In addition to repeating a word, they would repeat a particular concept in slightly different wording. When the apostle Paul was warning the Galatians not to abandon the biblical gospel, he said to them, "Even if we or an angel from heaven should preach to you a gospel contrary to what we have preached to you, a curse be on him!" (Gal. 1:8). Then the apostle added, "I now say again: If anyone is preaching to you a gospel contrary to what you received, a curse be on him!" (v. 9). Paul used the second form of Jewish repetition here, making the same point twice with slightly different words.

Jesus did the same. He first said, "Truly I tell you, unless someone is born again, he cannot see the kingdom of God" (John 3:3). Nicodemus replied: "How can anyone be born when he is old? . . . Can he enter his mother's womb a second time and be born?" (v. 4). Then Jesus responded, "Truly I tell you, unless someone is born of water and the Spirit, he cannot enter the kingdom of God" (v. 5). The Lord's repetition of this key requirement shows how essential it is.

Here's what we can know from the teaching of Jesus Christ: It is impossible to see the kingdom and to enter the kingdom unless one is born again.

If you have not been "born again," to whom could you turn to learn more about this? A pastor, friend, spouse, or coworker? Set an appointment with that person today!

THE SAMARITAN WOMAN

A Parched Follower

INTRODUCTION

We all have favorite people to talk with, such as a spouse, parent, or close friend. Conversations go all sorts of directions, but the best conversations often have an intentional goal—a purpose that seeks to help and improve one or both people. Jesus had this type of conversation with a woman in Samaria.

The Samaritan woman went to draw water from a well in the town of Sychar. Jesus happened to be traveling through the region and had stopped at the well. It was midday and most likely very hot. The conversation between Jesus and the woman would prove to be life-changing for her.

The Samaritan woman had a knowledge of religion. She knew about Old Testament characters like Jacob and Joseph. She was able to talk openly about worship. She knew about religious customs between her people and the Jews. But in spite of all her knowledge, she had a very questionable past. Her knowledge of religion had not made a difference in how she chose to live her life. Jesus would use that to His advantage to help her realize the great gift of salvation that He was able to offer her and her people, the Samaritans.

Were you ever told to avoid certain people when you were growing up? Did your parents ever tell you not to journey to certain parts of the city? Explain.

Why would Jesus choose to risk His reputation by openly engaging in a conversation with a woman in public—a practice that was taboo in His day?

Watch the video teaching for Session 3 to discover "The World of the Samaritan Woman," then continue the group discussion.

GROUP DISCUSSION

Focus Attention

How has our ability to converse with one another been positively or negatively impacted by the rise of social media and electronic methods of communication?

Explore The Text

As a group, read John 4:1-3.

Why would Jesus and His disciples leave Judea, where they were beginning to experience success in ministry?

As a group, read John 4:4-9.

Why do you think Jesus traveled through Samaria? What was strange about this?

As a group, read John 4:10-12.

In what ways did the woman misunderstand Jesus in His conversation with her?

As a group, read John 4:13-19.

How did Jesus begin to reveal His true self to the Samaritan woman?

As a group, read John 4:25-26 and John 4:27-30,39-42.

How did the Samaritan woman respond once Jesus revealed His true identity? What important things followed this revelation?

APPLY THE TEXT

Jesus broke cultural taboos in order to speak to a desperate woman trapped in a sinful lifestyle. She had led such a sinful life that she avoided public contact when possible, and on a day like any other day, she met Jesus. Without any condemnation on His part, Jesus offered the woman eternal life in Him, using words and terms she would understand that related to the task she was completing at the well. Jesus' offer of new, abundant life is not limited to Jews. He extends that offer to all people!

Do you feel as if there are reasons you aren't good enough for Jesus? How does this story speak against this feeling?

How can you use your testimony and salvation story to share the message of Christ?

In what people or things are you most tempted to look for fulfillment instead of looking to Christ? How can we hold one another accountable to look only to Christ this week?

Close your group time in prayer, reflecting on what you have discussed.

THE SAMARITAN WOMAN

KEY VERSE

Then the woman left her water jar, went into town, and told the people, "Come see a man who told me everything I ever did. Could this be the Messiah?"

— John 4:28

BASIC FACTS

1. Unidentified woman from the village of Sychar who had a life-changing conversation with Jesus when she came to draw water from the community well.

2. Descendant of an ethnically mixed population who were forcibly settled in the old Northern Kingdom of Israel (Samaria) by the Assyrians (2 Kings 17:24).

3. Unsuccessful in marriage; had five former husbands and yet lived with a sixth man outside of marriage.

4. No other biographical information for this woman given in Scripture.

TIMELINE

AD 30–40

- Jesus' ministry, crucifixion, resurrection, ascension 30–33
- Jesus encounters Samaritan woman at Sychar 31
- Birth of the church during Pentecost 33
- Stephen's martyrdom 33
- Conversion of Saul (Paul) 33

AD 40–50

- Herod Agrippa I rules in Judea 41–44
- Barnabas brings Paul to Antioch 43
- Paul's first missionary journey 47–48
- Jerusalem Council 49
- Claudius expels Jews from Rome 49

KNOWN FOR

1. All that is known about the Samaritan woman in Scripture is found in John 4:1-42.

2. First-century Jews typically despised the Samaritans, considering them impure, untrustworthy, and unworthy of life. Most Jews literally went out of their way to avoid any contact with Samaritans (John 4:9).

3. The Samaritan woman was shocked that Jesus, a Jewish man, would talk to her and request a drink of water from her.

4. When the woman realized that Jesus was the Messiah (4:25-26) and that He had living water to give her, she returned to her village and told the people about her encounter with Jesus. As a result, the townspeople went to see Jesus and invited Him to stay in their village for a time (4:40-41).

AD 50-60

- Paul's second missionary journey 50–52
- Paul's third missionary journey 53–57
- Antonius Felix governor of Judea 52–60
- Synoptic Gospels written 55–59
- Paul arrested in Jerusalem; sent to Rome 57–59

AD 60-70

- Paul under house arrest in Rome 61–62
- Apostle James martyred in Jerusalem 62
- Great fire in Rome 64
- Apostle Peter martyred in Rome 66
- Apostle Paul martyred in Rome 67

Breaking All the Rules: Jesus and the Samaritan Woman

By Rodney Reeves

No wonder Jesus constantly got in trouble. He believed people were more important than rules. Jesus' behavior enraged the Pharisees, who were known for keeping all the rules—not only the Law of God but also the commandments of men. Like any culture, society dictated certain things a person should and should not do.

Jesus seemed to break all the rules when He made a simple request of a Samaritan woman at Jacob's well (John 4:5-42). Indeed, Jesus was doing more than simply trying to quench His thirst when He asked the Samaritan woman for water. He was defying the stereotypes that divided people—then and now—believing that our common need of a Savior would unite all people, whether Jews or Samaritans, male or female, righteous or sinners.

Jesus did more than ignore centuries of ethnic hostilities when He, a Jewish man, asked the Samaritan woman for a drink of water. Jesus' request startled the woman (John 4:9), for men and women seldom engaged in public conversation. The reason a man would approach an unknown woman in public typically would be to initiate an improper relationship. To her way of thinking, a strange man traveling alone was probably looking for some company. So, when Jesus said, "Go, call your husband," the woman would have taken the comment as an inquiry into her availability. Indeed, when she responded, "I have no husband," she was signaling her willingness to take the next step in this potentially salacious encounter (see vv. 16,17, NASB). She had no idea, though, whom she was addressing.

After Jesus revealed the details of her troubled past, the Samaritan woman realized this was no ordinary man (v. 19). She may have thought to herself, *He's a Jew; I'm a Samaritan. He's a man; I'm a woman. He's a prophet; I'm a sinner. Why in the world would He ask me for a drink?* In their day, a holy man would never risk defilement by drinking from an unclean bucket—a vessel that belonged to an unclean, immoral, Samaritan woman. By His willingness to drink from her bucket, Jesus was essentially saying that she was a clean vessel too. That must have become ever more apparent when He treated her theological questions with respect.

Jacob's well at Sychar.

Overview of Shechem with Mount Ebal in the background. Shechem, which translates as "shoulders" in Hebrew, is located between two mountains, Mounts Ebal and Gerizim. Shechem and Sychar were both part of the same ancient settlement; the word "Sychar" was likely a derivation of the word "Shechem." Jacob made his home here; his well is located at Sychar.

Jesus thus treated this immoral, Samaritan woman as if she were just as important to God as a Jewish holy man. He made clear to her that all people, whether Jew or Samaritan, man or woman, clean or unclean, are invited to worship the one, living, true God.

That was why Jesus shared His identity with her. And that was why she ran into her town bragging about the man she met at Jacob's well. She drank deeply from the well of living water. She found the Messiah. And, just as Jesus predicted, from her sprang up living water, bringing life to some Samaritans who came to believe that Jesus, a Jewish man, is the "Savior of the world" (v. 42).

Why did this happen? Because Jesus knows that, regardless of who we are on the outside and despite the rules that separate us, deep down we are all the same. We are individuals who need a Savior.

Rodney Reeves, "Breaking All the Rules: Jesus and the Samaritan Woman," *Biblical Illustrator,* Fall 2012.

Read John 4:1-26.

The Pharisees had investigated John the Baptist's credentials; now they were looking into those of Jesus. His success in attracting new followers, and the fact that His disciples were baptizing them in greater numbers than John the Baptist, worried the Jewish religious leaders. As Jesus left Jerusalem, He chose to go through Samaria. This was not the typical path for a Jew; the usual route was to go down to Jericho and then follow the Jordan River north to Galilee. As Jesus and the disciples journeyed, they came to a stopping point around noon close to the Samaritan village of Sychar. Tired from the journey, Jesus stayed at a well while the disciples went into town to buy food. At the well, Jesus encountered a Samaritan woman. Typically women gathered their water in the morning when it was cool; this woman was at the well in the middle of the day. She was avoiding the other women for some reason.

Jesus engaged the woman in a conversation. He first asked for water, then offered her living water. Living water meant that she would never thirst again. It was the promise of an abundant life that so many people desire. She asked Him how He could give living water, asking if He was greater than Jacob who dug the well. Jesus was referring to eternal life, however the woman wanted a water that kept her from going back to the well. She didn't yet understand who Jesus was or what He really meant.

When have you been confused about a teaching in the Bible? How did you come to finally understand it?

Jesus changed the conversation, asking to speak to the woman's husband. She didn't have a husband. In actuality, she had been married five times and was now living with a man who was not her husband. This would have caused her fellow townspeople to consider her an extremely sinful person—someone to shun and avoid. Her motive for coming to the well at noon was clear. She needed water but didn't need the condemnation of her fellow townspeople. She journeyed to the well at a time of day when no one should have been there.

She sensed Jesus was powerful and wise, and called Him a prophet from God. She asked Him about the correct place of worship. Jesus changed her way of thinking by telling her that soon God would dwell in people, not temples or mountains. Everywhere would be a place of true worship. After hearing this, Jesus revealed His true identity to her. He told her He was the Messiah, the One who would come to teach and reveal God to the people.

Because the Holy Spirit lives in every believer, we can worship Him anywhere and at any time. Where has been your favorite place of worship, one where you felt a special connection to God?

In what ways have you misunderstood Jesus' true nature and identity as God's Son? How did you grow in your understanding?

Read John 4:4-10.

"He had to travel through Samaria" (v. 4). What a world of meaning there is in that phrase. Jesus didn't need to save the three days He could gain by passing through this ill-regarded province rather than crossing the river and going up the eastern desert route. There didn't seem to be urgent needs in Galilee that would cause Him to shorten the journey.

Jesus knew the ignorance and spiritual hunger of the Samaritan people, and the Father had sent Him into the whole world—not just part of it. He couldn't avoid these people in spite of the long history of resentment and antagonism between Jews and Samaritans.

Are there any types of people with whom you avoid interacting? Explain.

Any Jew could give perfectly valid reasons for this anger and separation. After all, the Samaritans were descendants of those who had not been deported or killed in the fall of the Northern Kingdom in 722 BC (see 2 Kings 17:23-40). These survivors had intermarried with the heathen colonists brought in from Babylonia by the Assyrian conquerors. So these people were looked upon as unclean traitors to Jewish blood.

Furthermore, the Samaritans were confused, even heretical in their religious beliefs. Even though their earlier polytheistic worship, caused by strangers bringing in their own gods, had given way to the worship of Jehovah, they accepted only the five books of Moses as their Scriptures and cut themselves off from the riches of the rest of the Old Testament.

Who in your life worships differently than you? Believes differently than you? How so?

All the makings of a dramatic confrontation were present as the woman approached the well. But the wearied Jesus only made a simple, unexpected request of her. "Give me a drink" (v. 7). In quietly asking her for help, Jesus cut through centuries of suspicion and animosity. This breakthrough was not the outcome of a conference on cross-cultural evangelism. No, there simply had been the honest expression of a basic human need. And at a deeper level, there had been the loving concern of one reaching out to touch that other solitary, needy person.

The woman could only respond with undisguised amazement, "How is it that you, a Jew, ask for a drink from me, a Samaritan woman?" (v. 9). Jesus had disarmed her. She didn't throw up a wall of defensiveness, but rather invited some kind of explanation. With the phrase, "For Jews do not associate with Samaritans," John sought to help us understand what a wide, deep chasm Jesus had come to bridge.

The One who asked for water is Himself the Giver of the everlasting water of life. And the one who is asked is in desperate need of the water that the Stranger alone could give. How strange and beautiful that the Giver of living water had come in weakness to share God's gift. What would happen if we let Jesus teach us about reaching out in our neighborhoods and to our coworkers, becoming transparent and open, being less imperialistic and arrogant, and more humble and real in our approach to people?

There is "living water" that is the "gift of God," and it can be this woman's for the asking. Gift! What a beautiful word of generosity and grace. Out of His rich bounty God shares all He has. But the Gift cannot be received without the Giver. "If you knew the gift of God, and who is saying to you, 'Give me a drink,' you would ask him, and he would give you living water" (v. 10). Jesus sought to penetrate the woman's spiritual darkness. Unless she came to know and accept the One who spoke to her, His gift could never be hers.

Have you asked God to give you the gift of eternal life, the living water He promised to the Samaritan woman? With whom can you talk to find out more?

Read John 4:27-42.

The disciples had been in town buying groceries during Jesus' conversation with the woman, but now they returned. Since it was midday, they urged Jesus to have some lunch. The disciples would naturally have been surprised to find Jesus talking with a woman—especially a Samaritan woman (Jews considered Samaritans ceremonially unclean). Spiritual sensitivity, a sense of courtesy, and Jesus' example may have helped the disciples overcome their natural Jewish revulsion at this predicament.

A change in the woman is evident in verses 28-29. First, she had come to draw water, but she was so excited that she abandoned her water jar. Second, she rushed back into town and exclaimed the revelations of her personal life when, just a short time ago, she had come to the well alone, quite likely as a social outcast. Third, on the basis of Jesus' omniscience, she raised the question of whether the Messiah had come.

When have you seen someone experience a dramatic change because they trusted Christ to be their Savior? How did the person change?

If you were a townsperson who knew the sinful woman before she met Christ at the well, what might you have thought or felt when you saw her excitement and enthusiasm about Jesus?

The story of Jesus' disciples' perception begins in verse 27, and is returned to in verse 31. John, the writer of this gospel, wanted to help the reader understand how Jesus brought His disciples to accept the universal nature of His mission. Jesus came to save all people, not just the Jews. John used the disciple's search for food to illustrate a great truth that we don't want to miss. The major concern of the disciples in the story was their search for food—undoubtedly kosher food. So their invitation for Jesus to eat is a reflection of their concern. By contrast, the primary focus of Jesus was hardly on food; it was the search for people.

Accordingly, Jesus responded to their request that He should eat by indicating He had a source of food that was unknown to them. The follow-up statement that Jesus' food was doing the will of the One who sent Him, reasserts the theme that Jesus was on a mission as an agent of God doing the Father's will. Jesus' words about the harvest are built around two statements that are almost proverbial in nature. The first concerns the timing of harvest. The text represents a general Palestinian proverbial statement concerning the time between sowing and the earliest point of harvest. It was already harvest time, and the disciples should have been ready for it (v. 35). Jesus wanted them, and us, to understand that people are ready to respond to the gospel now.

How should Jesus' example of searching for spiritually lost people impact our daily lives? Who in your circle of friends and acquaintances might be ready to learn more about Jesus?

We already know the woman had a change of heart and mind that indicated new birth. She had gone back to town to announce her meeting with Jesus. John reported that many Samaritans believed that day because of the woman's testimony. But since this is one of John's key words, he wanted to emphasize what actually happened in that town. Preliminary faith that rested on the woman's testimony became solid faith after the Savior stayed there two days and proclaimed His message.

How did Jesus witness? He was friendly; He asked questions; He showed concern for human need; He faithfully explained the Scriptures; and He emphasized good news for thirsty people. Witnesses aren't responsible for converting people; their task is to tell the truth about what they know.

Is there anything keeping you from witnessing for Christ? If so, then what is it?

MARY, MARTHA, AND LAZARUS

A Family of Followers

INTRODUCTION

Entertaining people in your home can either drain you of strength because of all the details and preparation, or you can draw energy from it, knowing that you are serving others by creating an experience they won't soon forget. Shopping for groceries, cleaning the house, and creating a nice evening for friends and family can be the highlight of a week or a holiday.

This is just one kind of busyness that many of us encounter in the course of life. Perhaps your busyness doesn't come from entertaining, but from the daily grind of helping children complete homework or working late at the office to get a project completed for the boss. Sociologists have declared that most of us live what is referred to as "time-compressed lives." We are way too busy. We need rest. We need to give our attention to more important matters that restore us, not drain us.

Such was the issue for two sisters sharing an evening with Jesus and others. Martha and Mary had invited the Lord to their home. During His visit, one of the sisters moved about the home constantly: cleaning, cooking, and preparing for their guests. The other sister chose a slightly different approach, and it caused friction in their relationship. Jesus would soon set them straight, and teach them what was truly important.

If you had a night to rest and relax, how would you spend it?

Why do we let our schedules get so busy these days? What motivates us to always be at work?

Watch the video teaching for Session 4 to discover "The World of Mary, Martha, and Lazarus," then continue the group discussion.

GROUP DISCUSSION

FOCUS ATTENTION

How would you describe your personality? Who do you take after more—your father or mother? How are you similar to or different from your siblings?

EXPLORE THE TEXT

As a group, read Luke 10:38-42.

What was Jesus trying to help Martha understand by his statements in verses 41-42? What lessons can we learn from this encounter?

Martha's relationships with Jesus and her sister were strained because of her distractions and cares about creating the "perfect" evening. What is the warning for us?

As a group, read John 11:1-6,11-14.

What additional information do you get about Mary, Martha, and Lazarus from these verses?

How do you explain the apparent discrepancy in Jesus' words about Lazarus in verses 4 and 11-14?

As a group, read John 11:17-27.

How was Martha's response to Jesus' arrival and her stated beliefs both on target and slightly off target?

As a group, read John 11:38-44.

Why was Jesus so moved by the death of Lazarus?

APPLY THE TEXT

One of the clearest lessons in the Bible comes from the story of Martha, Mary, and Lazarus. Lazarus had the distinct understanding of what it was like to be dead, and yet alive, because of Jesus. Martha made a bold profession of faith. Mary worshiped Jesus with an expensive boldness.

When we concentrate on Jesus first, we discover that we are never truly alone or without help. We experience that His grace is sufficient for all that we face. And we find inner peace and strength to face whatever comes our way.

What different forms of busyness take over in your life?

What kinds of things in your life—even seemingly "spiritual" things—might distract you from choosing intimacy with Jesus over activity?

What situation are you facing today that seems insurmountable? Based on Jesus' power over death and the grave, is there any reason that Jesus couldn't provide deliverance for you?

Close your group time in prayer, reflecting on what you have discussed.

MARY, MARTHA, AND LAZARUS

KEY VERSES

The Lord answered her, "Martha, Martha, you are worried and upset about many things, but one thing is necessary. Mary has made the right choice, and it will not be taken away from her."

— Luke 10:41-42

BASIC FACTS

1. Two Jewish sisters who, along with their brother Lazarus, sometimes hosted Jesus in their home in Bethany.

2. Name *Mary* is a short form of *Miriam*, meaning of which is uncertain.

3. Name *Martha* means "lady [of the house]," perhaps suggesting she was the older sister and owner of the house.

4. No information in Scripture as to whether either sister was ever married.

5. Name *Lazarus* means "one who God helps."

TIMELINE

AD 30–40

- Jesus' ministry, crucifixion, resurrection, ascension 30–33
- Siblings Mary, Martha, and Lazarus befriend Jesus 31
- Birth of the church during Pentecost 33
- Stephen's martyrdom 33
- Conversion of Saul (Paul) 33

AD 40–50

- Herod Agrippa I rules in Judea 41–44
- Barnabas brings Paul to Antioch 43
- Paul's first missionary journey 47–48
- Jerusalem Council 49
- Claudius expels Jews from Rome 49

KNOWN FOR

1. Mary received Jesus' commendation for giving priority to listening to Him teach about the things of God (Luke 10:39,42).

2. Mary anointed Jesus' feet with expensive perfume when He was about to enter Jerusalem for His final week on earth (John 12:3).

3. Mary and Martha sent word for Jesus to come to their house when their brother Lazarus was dying. Lazarus died and was buried before Jesus arrived, but Jesus brought him back to life, deepening the sisters' faith in Jesus as the Messiah (John 11:1-44).

4. Martha was concerned with meeting the obligations of a hostess, whether in preparing a meal (Luke 10:40) or serving her house guests (John 12:2).]

5. The name "Lazarus" appears in the New Testament only in John 11 and 12. The name is likely an abbreviated form of the more familiar Hebrew name "Eleazar," which means "God assists."

6. This Lazarus lived in Bethany, which tradition has identified with a site just east of the Kidron Valley and the Mount of Olives.

AD 50–60

- Paul's second missionary journey 50–52
- Paul's third missionary journey 53–57
- Antonius Felix governor of Judea 52–60
- Synoptic Gospels written 55–59
- Paul arrested in Jerusalem; sent to Rome 57–59

AD 60–70

- Paul under house arrest in Rome 61–62
- Apostle James martyred In Jerusalem 62
- Great fire in Rome 64
- Apostle Peter martyred in Rome 66
- Apostle Paul martyred in Rome 67

Lazarus Has Died

By Bobby Kelly

John's Gospel divides easily into the book of signs (John 1–11) and the book of glory (John 12–21). The book of signs is characterized by seven miracles or "signs" that serve to (1) indicate that Jesus is the Messiah, the Son of God, and (2) arouse faith in those who witness them. The raising of Lazarus marks the pivotal and climactic scene in the first half of John's Gospel and looks forward to the climactic scene of the entire Gospel, Jesus' resurrection.

John's Gospel details a close relationship between Jesus and Lazarus, Mary, and Martha. Clearly these siblings loved each other and loved Jesus deeply, and Jesus returned that love. Lazarus, Mary, and Martha lived in the village of Bethany, which was on the eastern slope of the Mount of Olives less than two miles east of Jerusalem.

The love, concern, and grief that Mary and Martha expressed for their brother's illness and eventual death drove the sisters to send for Jesus despite the danger Bethany posed for Him due to both its close proximity to Jerusalem and His increasingly antagonistic enemies (see 11:3,7-8). Surprisingly, Jesus delayed two days; Lazarus was already dead when He arrived (vv. 4-14).

Twice John stated that Lazarus had been dead for four days by the time Jesus arrived (vv. 17,39). Jesus intentionally delayed so that four days would pass before He arrived in Bethany. He did this so that He and the Father might be glorified (see v. 4). But why not go immediately and either heal Lazarus's illness or raise him after one, two, or even three days?

Underlying the story is the Jewish belief that the soul lingered around the body for three days after death hoping to re-enter. When the body began to decay and smell, the soul departed. Thus, Jesus waited until after the third day when Mary, Martha, and the others at Bethany would have given up all hope that somehow Lazarus might come back to life. Not only was Lazarus's body dead and beginning to decompose, but the spirit that animated the body and gave it life had reached the point of no possible return. [1]

Interior of the tomb of Lazarus. Visitors descend 24 steps (shown partially on the left) and enter a vestibule. Once inside the vestibule, three more steps lead down, through the rectangular hole in the floor, to the crypt where Lazarus's body was placed. According to tradition, Jesus stood in this vestibule area when He called Lazarus forth from the grave.

Illustrator Photo/
Brent Bruce (60/0895)

At the end of the book of signs, Jesus raised Lazarus from the dead. In time, though, Lazarus would die again. What a contrast to the end of the book of glory, one in which the Messiah would walk victoriously out of the grave alive. In contrast to Lazarus, Jesus would never face the grave again. Because of Jesus' resurrection, death has been defeated. Believers through the centuries have thus rejoiced and continue to do so because He was (and is) alive forevermore.

1. Craig A. Evans, *Jesus and the Ossuaries* (Waco: Baylor University Press, 2003), 14. See also Gerald L. Borchert, *John 1-11*, vol. 25a in The New American Commentary (Nashville: Broadman & Holman, 1996), 354.

Bobby Kelly, "Lazarus Has Died," *Biblical Illustrator,* Fall 2013.

Read Luke 10:38-42.

According to John 11–12, Mary and Martha lived in Bethany, which lies on the eastern slope of the Mount of Olives. The city is mentioned in Luke 19:29. A woman named Martha opened her home. The term "opened" or "welcomed" is also found in 19:6 and Acts 17:7. The name *Martha* is the feminine form of the Aramaic term *Mar* and means "mistress." Martha appears to have been the mistress in charge of the house.

Luke alone records this incident. The story emphasizes that quiet dependence on Jesus is more important than bustling service. Dedication to Jesus takes precedence over all other responsibilities and obligations. That's a much needed reminder in today's world!

John 11:1 and 12:1-3 locate Mary and Martha in Bethany. Luke simply placed them in a village. Location wasn't important for him. Response to Jesus was. Martha responded in the typical homeowner's way: fulfilling the social obligations.

Martha was busy preparing food and getting things ready for a night with the Savior. Her sister Mary responded in a different way. The rabbis taught people to listen to wise men or teachers but not to talk much with women. Jesus, the wisest of men, welcomed Mary to His audience of learners. Rather than helping her sister Martha with the preparations, Mary chose to sit and listen to Jesus.

When have you found rest in Jesus by spending time with Him? Where were you? What do you remember about your time?

Social obligations finally got the best of Martha, especially when her sister proved to be no help. Rather than inviting her sister to help, Martha went straight to Jesus for authority to force her sister to work.

For once, a person in need didn't receive Christ's blessing. The need was out of focus and misplaced. Martha was too stressed out about earthly things. Her life was dedicated to fulfilling the world's expectations rather than those of Jesus.

We have one essential need: to hear and obey the Word of God. Mary made the right choice. Jesus would not take away from her the blessing and opportunity. At the crossroads of decision making, Martha opted for worldly expectation and social obligation; Mary, for hearing Christ's Word. Martha needed to change her priorities. Jesus' message is the same to everyone everywhere: In all your busyness, don't forget that only one thing is necessary. That one thing is not the next task on your to-do list. That one thing is not serving others. The one necessary thing is enjoying the Lord Himself.

That's what Mary chose. Jesus calls it "the right choice." And "it will not be taken away from her" (v. 42). The use of the word "choice" is interesting. It's related to the lawyer's use of the word "inherit" in verse 25. Throughout the Bible, God says that He is the "portion" or "inheritance" of His people.

Jesus demands more than listening to His teaching and agreeing with what He says; He places us at the crossroads of life and forces us to decide to live His way or the world's way.

In today's "time-compressed" world, how do we slow down and spend an appropriate amount of time with the Lord each day?

Read John 11:1-14.

The name "Lazarus" appears in the New Testament only in John 11 and 12. The name is likely an abbreviated form of the more familiar Hebrew name "Eleazar," which means "God assists." In Lazarus's story, the grace of God is made evident through divine assistance.

The Lazarus in this story lived in Bethany, which tradition has identified with a site just east of the Kidron Valley and the Mount of Olives. The sisters, Mary and Martha, also are mentioned in this story. In this present context an interesting technique of storytelling is employed. Mary, the sister of Lazarus, is identified here before the event as the one who anointed the Lord and wiped His feet with her hair (see 11:2; 12:3). That loving, sacrificial event must have seared itself into the minds of the early Christians, as both Mark (see 14:9) and Matthew (see 26:13) bear witness.

The text indicates that the sisters were anxious for their brother's welfare and sent a message to Jesus. When Jesus received the message, He indicated that the end result would not be what it appeared to be—namely, "This sickness will not end in death"—but that through it both God and the Son of God would "be glorified" (11:4). The meaning of this text is multidimensional. It can be understood on several levels. One sense is that the death of Lazarus was not to be the end of the story, but the glory of God would be evidenced in that Jesus was about to bring him back from the dead.

If Jesus really loved Lazarus and his sisters (see 11:5), the reader is certainly tempted to ask, *Why did Jesus delay two more days and put the sisters through the agony of their brother's death?* Was Jesus a mean and thoughtless person? Humans generally interpret any delay in rendering help as cruel because of our perspectives on the avoidance of all pain and because of our general commitment to the immediacy of action as it pertains to time. But cruelty is hardly what this story is about.

When have you felt like Jesus has delayed responding to an important situation in your life?

When one reviews the time sequences in the story, it is quite possible that Lazarus was dead by the time Jesus received the message. By the time Jesus reached the tomb, the text says that Lazarus had been dead four days (11:39). Given the two-day delay and the time for travel, both of the messenger and of Jesus, it is not impossible that the sick man could have died while the messenger was en route.

Jesus' intention was to go and wake His sleeping friend, Lazarus (see 11:11). The disciples' fearful reply, however, was in fact a plea that He should avoid doing anything rash because sleeping and sick people usually wake up and get well. The disciples were about to experience more than they had anticipated in their understanding of the situation. The issue here was not, as they learned, one of natural sleep or general illness from which recovery can be expected because of normal processes (11:13). Instead, Lazarus was dead. Jesus faced that reality squarely.

Death and illness are not friendly human phenomena. Paul spoke of death as the last great enemy (see 1 Cor. 15:26; Rev. 20:14). To deal with that "last" enemy requires the Lord of life. Jesus told His disciples that He was glad He hadn't been at the bedside of Lazarus, because what was about to happen would greatly enhance their believing (see 11:15). Jesus was on the verge of showing His disciples, Mary and Martha, and all of the mourners who were present, that He is the Lord of life with power over death and the grave.

What encouragement can we take from this story? How can believers today draw strength when facing difficult circumstances?

Read John 11:17-27,38-44.

Lazarus had been dead four days. This fact was extremely important to those familiar with Jewish burial customs. The general belief was that the spirit of the deceased hovered around the body for three days in anticipation of some possible means of reentry into the body. But on the third day it was believed that the body lost its color, and the spirit was locked out. Therefore, the spirit was obliged to enter the chambers of Sheol (the place of the dead). The passing of the third day signaled the conclusion of the last modicum of hope for the mourners. The situation was one of hopelessness now. If only Jesus had arrived a day or two earlier!

When word got to Martha that Jesus was on His way, she arose and went out to meet Him. Mary, however, remained "seated in the house." The custom was for the bereaved to remain seated in the house and for the guests to come and sit in silence and periodically support the grieving parties with sympathetic tears and moans.

Martha expressed the deep emotions of that experience: "Lord, if you had been here" (v. 21). Those words were hardly a condemnation of Jesus for not being present when Lazarus was ill. The stark reality of this fact becomes clear almost immediately. The words are those of a grieving person who desperately wished it could have been different, but who recognized that the inevitable had come to pass. Moreover, her subsequent words, "even now" (11:22), must not be read as her belief that Jesus could reverse the reality of death (11:39). Instead, her statement should be understood as indicating a strong confidence in Jesus' relationship with the Father and that in spite of her resignation to Lazarus's death, somehow Jesus would understand the plight of the mourning sisters as well as the general nature of Lazarus's future hope.

When a loved one died, what brought you peace and comfort during that difficult time?

Resurrection and life were two related dimensions of Jesus' proclamation. Jesus clearly possesses the power of resurrection so that the one who believes in Jesus, even though he were to die, will experience that power of resurrection ("will live," 11:25) in their dead bodies. But beyond resurrection, Jesus is also life. Accordingly, whoever experiences resurrection ("lives and believes," 11:26), also will experience eternal life (see 3:16) and will never die (see 11:26; 3:16). Martha's brother was dead, and even though he had entered Sheol (the four days), he was not beyond the range of Jesus' power. Martha was in for a surprise.

The world was about to receive a taste of God's matchless power and grace that would conclude Jesus' public acts of power and point beyond the event to His own resurrection. It would forever mark Him as entirely unique. When Jesus' prayer ended at the tomb, Jesus yelled for the dead man to come from the tomb. This command of Jesus, "Lazarus, come out!" (11:43), is indicative of His supreme power over death. Imagine the reaction of those people as the body all wrapped in burial clothes stirred, rose out of the vault, and shuffled toward the mourners. When Lazarus came struggling forth, he was bound in the grave wrappings. So the third and final command of Jesus was to set him free of the bindings—to let him get out of the hindrances and be on his way (see 11:44).

Since Jesus has power over death and the grave, is there any circumstance in which He could not provide help and relief to you or a loved one? How can you keep Jesus' power in mind each time you face a trying or difficult experience?

THOMAS

A Doubting Follower

INTRODUCTION

Many of us operate under the mindset that "seeing is believing." We will believe something if we experience it. Until then, skepticism reigns.

Thomas is one of those skeptical followers of Jesus. He is often referred to as "Doubting Thomas" because he initially doubted the reports that Jesus was alive after His brutal crucifixion at the hands of the Jewish religious leaders and Romans.

The disciples gathered in a room and locked the door. Women had reported earlier that day that Jesus' body was no longer in the tomb. The disciples were fearful, and they were few. It wasn't long until Jesus appeared at their meeting and revealed Himself to them. They were overjoyed that their leader was alive.

But one disciple, Thomas, wasn't present. Thomas wasn't there when Jesus showed His disciples the scars from the crucifixion. When the disciples found Thomas and told him Jesus was alive, Thomas responded, "If I don't see the mark of the nails in his hands, put my finger into the mark of the nails, and put my hand into his side, I will never believe" (John 20:25).

Ultimately, Thomas did believe that Jesus was the Christ, the Messiah. But he didn't come to that conclusion until Jesus showed him His wounds, proving that it was really Him. Today, we must believe on the basis of faith; we may never see Jesus' wounds with our own eyes, yet we can believe that He rose from the dead and is who He claims to be.

Would you describe yourself as a skeptic or as a faith-filled follower of Jesus? Explain.

What is your biggest question about God or His work in the world?

Watch the video teaching for Session 5 to discover "The World of Thomas," then continue the group discussion.

Focus Attention

When have you experienced a period of doubt with regard to your faith? What were the circumstances?

Explore The Text

As a group, read John 20:19.

Based on verse 19 alone, what can we surmise about the disciples?

As a group, read John 20:20-23.

According to Luke 24:37, the disciples believed they were seeing a ghost. How did Jesus' response to their fears disprove this idea?

What things do you notice about Jesus' commission of His disciples in verses 21-22?

As a group, read John 20:24-31.

Thomas was absent from the gathering where Jesus revealed Himself to the disciples. Why might he have been so adamant about seeing Jesus for himself?

How does Thomas's response in verse 25, and Jesus' statement that follows, apply to us today?

APPLY THE TEXT

Thomas walked beside Jesus for three years. He heard Christ's teachings and saw Him perform many miracles, but he still struggled to believe Jesus had risen from the grave. We don't have the luxury of walking with Jesus or touching His scars. We live thousands of years removed from the events recorded in the Gospels, and Jesus recognizes the faith that it takes for us to believe.

Where could you use Jesus' peace right now?

What doubts or questions about God are you struggling with today?

Have you received the gift of the Holy Spirit? How has He changed you?

Close your group time in prayer, reflecting on what you have discussed.

THOMAS

KEY VERSE

Then he said to Thomas, "Put your finger here and look at my hands. Reach out your hand and put it into my side. Don't be faithless, but believe."

—John 20:27

BASIC FACTS

1. One of Jesus' twelve apostles who was initially skeptical about the resurrection but later convinced.

2. Name *Thomas* is of Aramaic origin, meaning "twin"; Greek equivalent is Didymus [DID ih muhs].

3. No information given in Scripture about either his twin sibling or other family members.

4. According to church tradition, may have died a martyr's death after the ascension as he proclaimed the gospel in India.

TIMELINE

AD 30–40

- Jesus' ministry, crucifixion, resurrection, ascension 30–33
- Thomas follows Jesus; becomes an apostle 30
- Birth of the church during Pentecost 33
- Stephen's martyrdom 33
- Conversion of Saul (Paul) 33

AD 40–50

- Herod Agrippa I rules in Judea 41–44
- Barnabas brings Paul to Antioch 43
- Paul's first missionary journey 47–48
- Jerusalem Council 49
- Claudius expels Jews from Rome 49

KNOWN FOR

1. Thomas is identified as being among the twelve apostles in the three Synoptic Gospels and Acts (Matt. 10:3; Mark 3:18; Luke 6:14; Acts 1:13). No specific account is given of Jesus' calling of Thomas as a disciple. John's Gospel provides several additional accounts of Thomas's activities.

2. When Jesus decided to return to Judea because of Lazarus's death, Thomas challenged the Twelve to accompany Jesus even if it resulted in their deaths (John 11:16).

3. Thomas expressed confusion about Jesus' teaching that He was going away to prepare a place for His followers and would return one day to get them (John 14:5).

4. Thomas initially refused to believe the testimony of other disciples who claimed they had seen the risen Lord Jesus, contending that he would believe only if he was able to see and touch the resurrected Lord (John 20:24-25). For this skepticism, Thomas was referred to by many Christians of a later era as "Doubting Thomas."

5. When the risen Christ appeared to the gathered disciples (including Thomas) a week later, Thomas touched Jesus' body and declared his confident faith in Jesus as his Lord and God (John 20:26-29).

6. Thomas joined a group of seven disciples who went fishing on the Sea of Galilee and encountered the risen Lord Jesus. Jesus and His disciples baked and ate some of the fish caught, and Jesus restored Simon Peter to a role of leadership (John 21:1-19).

AD 50–60

- Paul's second missionary journey 50–52
- Paul's third missionary journey 53–57
- Antonius Felix governor of Judea 52–60
- Synoptic Gospels written 55–59
- Paul arrested in Jerusalem; sent to Rome 57–59

AD 60–70

- Paul under house arrest in Rome 61–62
- Apostle James martyred In Jerusalem 62
- Great fire in Rome 64
- Apostle Peter martyred in Rome 66
- Apostle Paul martyred in Rome 67

Thomas in Scripture

By Timothy N. Boyd

The majority of what we know about Jesus' disciples involves His inner circle, Peter, James, and John. Another of the apostles, though, stands out because of his insistence of knowing with certainty.

Thomas is one of the best known of the apostles because of one incident that occurred after Jesus' resurrection (see John 20:24-29). Thomas had not been present when the resurrected Christ originally presented Himself to the disciples. Unwilling to take their word for it, Thomas declared he was not willing to believe that Jesus was resurrected until he could physically touch Christ's wounds. Eight days after this declaration, Jesus again appeared to the disciples—this time Thomas was present. Jesus allowed Thomas to touch His wounds and challenged him to believe and cease his disbelief. Thomas immediately confessed Christ as his Lord and God.

Even though Thomas believed, he would forever be known as "Doubting Thomas." In fact, "Doubting Thomas" has become a common description for anyone who experiences doubt in faith or in other parts of life. This moment was significant for more than the moment of doubt. It was one great moment that showed both the validity of Jesus' resurrection and the physical nature of His resurrected body. Thomas touched Him. He felt Jesus' flesh and knew the truth of His bodily resurrection.

While the incident in John 20:24-29 is the best-known reference to Thomas in the Gospels, he also came to the forefront in other portions of John's Gospel. The other Gospels and the Book of Acts mention Thomas in lists of the apostles, but he does not stand out from the crowd in those references.

John 11 records Jesus' receiving word about Lazarus's illness and subsequent death. He had been speaking to the disciples about His own coming death. The disciples had been expressing their own fears that the Jewish religious leaders wanted to stone Him. Yet, Jesus was determined to go to the home of His friend Lazarus. Thomas was the one who turned to the other disciples and encouraged them to accompany Jesus on this journey even if it meant their own deaths (v. 16). This demonstrated his own personal courage and commitment to Christ.

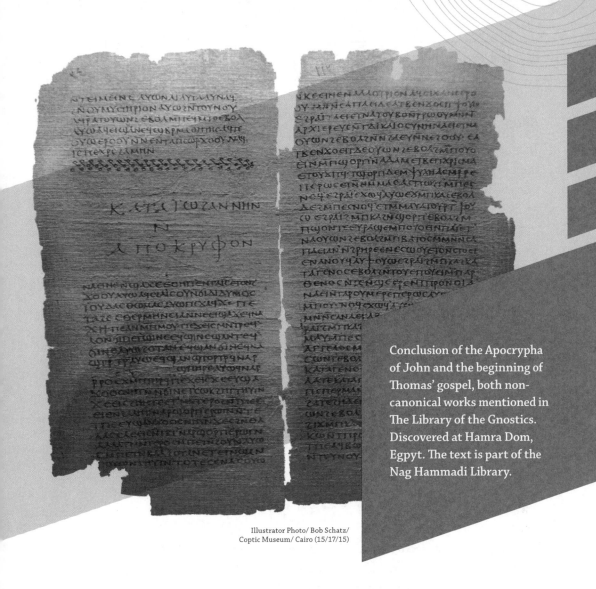

Conclusion of the Apocrypha of John and the beginning of Thomas' gospel, both non-canonical works mentioned in The Library of the Gnostics. Discovered at Hamra Dom, Egpyt. The text is part of the Nag Hammadi Library.

In John 14, Jesus was comforting His disciples about what His passion would mean for them. He told them that He was going to prepare a place for them and then return to take them to Himself. He added that they knew the way that He was going. John states that Thomas stepped to the fore and challenged Christ, "Lord, we do not know where You are going, how do we know the way?" (v. 5, NASB). Jesus replied that He *was* indeed the way.

What do these passages in the Gospel of John tell us about Thomas? He was blunt, honest, and willing to go against the other disciples in matters of personal conscience. He was also a person willing to admit he was wrong and to embrace the resurrected Christ in renewed faith.

Timothy N. Boyd, "Thomas in Scripture," *Biblical Illustrator*, Fall 2017.

Read John 20:24-26.

Thomas has often been vilified by Christians because of his early doubts expressed in these verses. But throughout the Gospel of John, he is presented as a realist, a person who evaluated situations on the basis of what he could perceive. He understood the dangers of going south to Judea (11:16), and he wanted more than words in order to follow Jesus to His place of preparation (14:5). But he was willing to take risks for Jesus, and in these verses he is also capable of reaching magnificent conclusions. Thomas is not merely a pathetic doubter. He is a paradigm for many Christians who are capable of great possibilities as well as hesitations in faith.

Thomas has been categorized as a "pessimist." In reality, he was more likely a realist. He needed proof positive before he would believe. He was open to the possibility of Jesus being alive, but it would take something spectacular to cause him to assent to it—something like seeing Jesus for himself.

What might keep a person from believing in Jesus? What do they need to see or experience before they believe?

The disciples who had experienced the surprising appearance of Jesus and His empowering commissioning were enthusiastically ready to share the details of their post-resurrection experience of the Lord. But like many of us who have experienced the marvel of transforming grace and desire to share it, these disciples were met with a cold, skeptical face. Thomas had not been at the meeting, and he had no immediate sense of the significance of the miracle that had occurred, an event that changed the course of history and would soon change his life as well.

What might have the disciples felt when Thomas refused to believe their report that Jesus was alive, and they had all seen him?

Thomas's only reaction at that in-between state was the human tendency to demand proof of such an incredible fact. His demand was for some assurance to connect in a reliable manner the physical Jesus of the crucifixion (His hands and His side) with the experience of the other disciples. After all, that is what they said they had been able to do (John 20:20).

Thomas's demand was to have virtually the same experience they had received, only in his case he wanted to "shove" (the Greek word *balo*) his finger into the place or holes made by the nails, and likewise to "shove" his hand into Jesus' side where the spear had been stuck. Unless he had such physical proof, he stated, "I will never believe [what you are saying]." Although this statement of Thomas may seem to be quite obstinate, there is a sense in which contemporary believers ought to thank God that someone like Thomas was there to do the reality check for us.

The next Lord's Day, Thomas was also present in the community meeting. The doors were once again shut tight. The early readers of John's Gospel must have clearly felt a kinship with the first believers, since they also were a marked group of people, excluded from synagogues and undoubtedly seized and imprisoned.

Do you have any current doubts about who Jesus is? What are those doubts?

Read John 20:27-29.

The story of Thomas has been compared to the story of Nathaniel at the beginning of the Gospel of John (see John 1:43-50). In both cases, the result is a powerful confession. In the Nathaniel story, however, Jesus informs the confessor that He will take the novice far beyond mere Jewish expectations of the coming of the Messiah (John 1:50-51). In the closing response of Jesus to Thomas, He will likewise take this novice disciple far beyond his human demands to a new view of believing.

It is most probable that when Thomas made his demand for proof, he hardly expected to have his material proof met. Similarly, when the early church prayed for Peter's release from prison, their reaction to the report clearly indicates their doubts about their own prayers (see Acts 12:13-15). These stories indicate that what often is viewed as believing and praying is, in fact, not much more than human wishful thinking.

What kinds of miracles does Jesus perform every day, yet people fail to acknowledge who He is or how He is at work?

Thomas's response forms the high point of confession in the Gospel. What it does is bring the Gospel full circle from where it is emphatically said that "the Word was God" (John 1:1) to this confession, "My Lord and my God" (John 20:20). The confession also touches directly upon the daily Jewish reciting of the Shema, "Hear, O Israel, the Lord our God, the Lord is one" (Deut 6:4). The early Christians thus claimed for Jesus attributes akin to Yahweh, the God of the Old Testament. To suggest that such a confession might go unnoticed by the Jews would be highly naive. Moreover, since the Roman Emperors took to themselves designations of divinity, it meant that the early Christians were caught in a grip between two hostile forces. This confession epitomizes the highest declaration Christians could make concerning Jesus and brought them into a direct challenge with their contemporaries.

There was one last part of the exchange between Thomas and the risen Jesus that needed to be communicated. John wrote to a community of believers who had never seen the risen Lord and whose witnesses to the historical presence of Jesus had for the most part died or were about to die. What he wrote, therefore, was in the form of both a rhetorical question and a concluding beatitude: "Because you have seen me, you have believed. Blessed are those who have not seen and yet believe" (v. 29). To this rhetorical question, the evangelist added that Jesus pronounced a beatitude upon those who were able to believe without such first-hand support or proof. This would have encouraged John's readers, for they had placed their faith and trust in Jesus, someone they had never met.

Who initially shared the gospel with you? did your response compare to Thomas's response?

Read John 20:30-31.

These twenty chapters of John are a masterpiece of literary construction. They are artistically designed like a symphony, yet pointedly focused; simplistically worded for the reader, yet intensely complex in meaning; and dramatically engaging in the stories, yet very deliberate in the speech presentation. The Gospel is a marvel of inspired writing. And its concluding two verses sum up its purpose in what has to be one of the great classic summations of biblical literature. Although the author, John, acknowledged that much had been left untold, the main point is clear: "Jesus performed many other signs in the presence of his disciples that are not written in this book. But these are written so that you may believe that Jesus is the Messiah, the Son of God, and that by believing you may have life in his name."

How does a sign strengthen a person's faith? What kinds of "signs" have you experienced?

John's mind went back. He began to recall miracle after miracle he had seen Jesus perform—more than he could count. Only thirty six are recorded in the Gospels (so few in relation to the total sum in order to de-emphasize miracles as a basis for faith), but John knew of many more. Out of that treasury he himself had selected only eight special signs to help him achieve his objective.

In John's day, a twofold attack was mounted against the person of Christ. There were those who emphasized His deity at the expense of His humanity. There were those who emphasized His humanity at the expense of His deity. To combat those heresies, John wrote two books: his Gospel and his first Epistle. In his Gospel, John shows that the Jesus of history was more than a mere man, He is the Son of God (as opposed to mere "flesh"). In his first Epistle, he shows that the Son of God was a true man (as opposed to mere "spirit").

Thomas had just confessed Jesus as God—absolutely, unconditionally, incontrovertibly God. And there are signs without number that Jesus of Nazareth was the Christ, the anointed of God, the promised Messiah of Israel, and God over all, blessed forevermore. To believe this is the basis of having "life through His name." His name here, "Christ, the Son of God," reveals His twofold nature.

Nothing less than a dynamic believing in the person of Jesus, who is both Christ and Son of God in the highest meaning of those terms, would be adequate for John. Moreover, nothing less than genuine believing that issues in life transformation would satisfy the evangelist's goal for writing this Gospel.

With such an initial summation, this work of John reaches its powerful conclusion. The evangelist, John, achieved his desire of presenting a captivating picture of the divine Word become flesh (1:14), so that humanity could behold the glory of the Father's/God's only Son (1:14,18). And from the incredible fullness of this Son, all who have placed faith in Christ have become the recipients of overwhelming grace (1:16).

If you have never placed your faith in Jesus, would you do that now? You can pray a simple prayer such as, "Dear Jesus, I believe you are who You say You are, and who the Bible presents You to be. I believe You are God's Son, and that You lived a sinless life, only to be put to death in my place. I believe that God brought You back to life, and that I can live with You forever because of that. Forgive me for not trusting in You until now. Thank You for hearing this prayer and for saving me from my sin. Amen."

If you prayed that prayer, please tell someone today! Notify a Christian friend or family member. Attend the worship service of a Bible-believing church in your city. Speak with the church's pastor and tell him that you want to know more about Jesus, and that you want to make others aware that you are a Christian by being baptized.

PETER

A Restored Follower

INTRODUCTION

Numerous television shows are centered on the practice of restoration. Some shows focus on the restoration of homes. Old floors are replaced, walls are torn down to make a home more open and airy, and new paint is always a must. Then there are shows that focus on the restoration of cars. Rust is removed, new parts are ordered, and a complete makeover takes place—all in the course of a one-hour show!

We're not only fascinated with things that are restored, but we are equally mesmerized when people are restored. Sometimes this happens when people lose a lot of weight. Other times restoration takes place relationally, between people who were previously estranged.

Peter, one of Jesus' disciples, failed Him miserably the night before His crucifixion. Peter denied knowing Jesus three times when asked whether or not he was one of Jesus' disciples. Jesus predicted this would happen, but Peter was sure it would not. Indeed it did happen, and Peter was left broken and in pieces. He needed restoration in the worst way.

What is the benefit of restoring things like houses and cars?

In what ways is the restoration of people similar to, but different from, the restoration of objects?

Watch the video teaching for Session 6 to discover "The World of Peter," then continue the group discussion.

FOCUS ATTENTION

What is something you have restored? How did you feel once the job was complete?

EXPLORE THE TEXT

As a group, read John 18:15-18.

How would you describe Peter in these verses?

As a group, read John 18:25-27.

What do you notice about Peter's second and third denials of Christ in these verses?

As a group, read John 21:1-7.

How did John recognize the Lord before announcing it to the rest of the disciples in the boat?

Why did Peter immediately jump into the water and swim to shore?

As a group, read John 21:15-22.

What is the significance of Jesus' three questions to Peter?

Why did Peter ask a question about the fate of John?

Apply The Text

Peter denied Jesus three times according to Jesus' prediction; it signaled an epic failure on the part of Peter, who was normally seen as very bold. But before we are too hard on Peter, we should examine our own lives. Are there times when you deny Jesus? The good news is that Jesus is willing to forgive you and place you back on solid ground. A failure is not fatal—it's only temporary. If you've failed the Lord, realize there is no condemnation from Him. He wants to restore you just as He restored Peter.

In what ways do you find yourself in need of restoration to God?

Where do you find encouragement in this story of Peter, his denial, and his restoration into ministry?

Peter told the Lord that he loved Him (three times). What might someone observe in your daily life that shows how much you love the Lord?

Close your group time in prayer, reflecting on what you have discussed.

PETER

KEY VERSE

He asked him the third time, "Simon, son of John, do you love me?" Peter was grieved that he asked him the third time, "Do you love me?" He said, "Lord, you know everything; you know that I love you." "Feed my sheep," Jesus said.

—John 21:17

BASIC FACTS

1. Early disciple of Jesus; one of the twelve apostles.

2. Name *Peter* is of Greek origin, meaning "rock"; known also in Scripture as Simon (from Hebrew Simeon, meaning "he has heard") and Cephas (Aramaic, meaning "rock").

3. Brother of the apostle Andrew and son of John (or Jonah); mother's name unknown.

4. A fisherman by trade until Jesus called him as a disciple.

5. Married; no children mentioned.

6. Hometown was Bethsaida but later lived in Capernaum.

7. Died a martyr's death in Rome; tradition holds he requested to be crucified upside down.

TIMELINE

AD 30–40

- Jesus' ministry, crucifixion, resurrection, ascension 30–33
- Simon Peter follows Jesus; becomes an apostle 30
- Birth of the church during Pentecost 33
- Stephen's martyrdom 33
- Conversion of Saul (Paul) 33

AD 40–50

- Herod Agrippa I rules in Judea 41–44
- Barnabas brings Paul to Antioch 43
- Paul's first missionary journey 47–48
- Jerusalem Council 49
- Claudius expels Jews from Rome 49

KNOWN FOR

1. Peter was introduced to Jesus by his brother, Andrew (John 1:40-42). Jesus called the two brothers to be His disciples as they were working in their fishing business (Mark 1:16-18).

2. Peter became a primary leader and spokesman for the disciples (Matt. 16:16; John 6:67-69) and later for the early church (Acts 1:15-22; 2:14-36; 15:7-11).

3. Often bold in his faith (John 18:10; Acts 4:13), Peter faltered terribly at times. He slept while he should have been praying in the garden of Gethsemane (Matt. 26:36-46). He denied knowing Jesus three times because of fear (Luke 22:54-62). He at times displayed an unwillingness to have open fellowship with Gentile believers (Acts 10:9-16; Gal. 2:11-12).

4. The risen Lord Jesus restored Peter to a leadership role in the gospel movement after confirming Peter's love and devotion to Him (John 21:15-19).

5. Peter preached a powerful sermon on the Day of Pentecost, after which at least 3,000 converts were baptized (Acts 2:14-41).

6. Peter proclaimed the gospel to a centurion and his household in Caesarea after having a vision in which the Lord confronted the apostle's prejudice against Gentiles (Acts 10:9-48).

7. Peter wrote two epistles in the New Testament, 1 and 2 Peter, that instruct believers on how to live as the people of God in a hostile environment.

AD 50-60

- Paul's second missionary journey 50–52
- Paul's third missionary journey 53–57
- Antonius Felix governor of Judea 52–60
- Synoptic Gospels written 55–59
- Paul arrested in Jerusalem; sent to Rome 57–59

AD 60-70

- Paul under house arrest in Rome 61–62
- Apostle James martyred In Jerusalem 62
- Great fire in Rome 64
- Apostle Peter martyred in Rome 66
- Apostle Paul martyred in Rome 67

Simon Peter's Ministry Assignment

By Jerry N. Barlow

Prior to the crucifixion, Jesus and His disciples gathered in Jerusalem to celebrate Passover (see Matt. 26:17-19). That night, however, Jesus made some startling statements (vv. 26-28). Jesus declared, "One of you will betray me" (v. 21). He later said, "Tonight all of you will fall away" (v. 31).

No doubt shaken by what Jesus said, Peter declared, "Even if everyone falls away . . . I will never fall away" (v. 33). Upon hearing that he would deny Jesus "three times," Peter exclaimed, "Even if I have to die with you . . . I will never deny you" (vv. 34-35).

Later, when troops came to apprehend Jesus in the garden, Peter drew his sword to defend Jesus (John 18:10). When Jesus stopped Peter, though, the disciples and Peter fled (Matt. 26:56), and the troops took Jesus to the high priest Caiaphas. Then, in the courtyard of Caiaphas, three times people confronted Peter about knowing and being with Jesus. Each time Peter denied such! When a rooster crowed after Peter's third denial, "He went outside and wept bitterly" (vv. 69-75).

Peter's Assignment

Following Peter's denials came Jesus' crucifixion and burial (see John 19:16-18,38-42). What a difficult time this must have been for those (including Peter) who had followed and loved Jesus. Great joy came, however, on the morning of Jesus' resurrection (Matt. 28:8)! That joy and wonder increased as Christ appeared to the disciples.

John 21 chronicles one of Jesus' post-resurrection appearances to His disciples (John 21:1,14). The chapter details Christ's conversation with Peter after breakfast (vv. 15-19). In that dialogue, why did Jesus ask Peter essentially the same question three times? And, why did Jesus direct Peter three times to a particular ministry assignment?

We notice how Jesus described Peter's ministry assignment: "Feed my lambs" (v. 15), "Shepherd my sheep" (v. 16), and "Feed my sheep" (v. 17). In essence, Peter's task was to emulate the ministry of Jesus, "the great Shepherd of the sheep" (Heb. 13:20), who lay down His life for His sheep (John 10:15).

Located in the Church of the Dormition, the Upper Room in Jerusalem. The room was restored in the 14th cent. using the upper parts of antique column shafts and capitals and adding a ogival vaulted ceiling from the Gothic period. The stone flooring is possibly, for the most part, from the original building. This is, according to tradition, the site of Jesus' last supper with His disciples.

Illustrator Photo/ Justin Veneman (63/0611)

Feeding Jesus' Sheep

What happened after Jesus' dialogue with Peter? The early chapters of the Book of Acts portray Peter boldly fulfilling his ministry assignment (see Acts 1–5; 9–12). He proclaimed the gospel at Pentecost. He was later persecuted and imprisoned for his continued preaching. He was the first apostle to bring Gentiles into the church. In 1 Corinthians, Paul mentioned some who tied their Christian lineage to Peter (1 Cor. 1:12; 3:22). These likely had Gentile backgrounds.

Peter's two epistles, which he probably wrote while in Rome, portray his heart as a shepherd. His encouragement, instructions, and even warnings in those letters offered instructions to early believers. He considered himself a fellow-elder and instructed the early church leaders to "Shepherd God's flock" (1 Pet. 5:2-3). In life examples recorded in Scripture and through his two epistles, Peter has for centuries continued to fulfill his assignment to feed Jesus' sheep.

Jerry N. Barlow, "Simon Peter's Ministry Assignment," *Biblical Illustrator,* Summer 2017.

Read Matthew 26:69-71; Mark 14:71.

Peter should never have been where he was among the enemies of Jesus Christ. That was the wrong place for a man like Peter. He denied the Lord by where he was. He had the wrong associates around him. David said, "How happy is the one who does not walk in the advice of the wicked" (Ps. 1:1). Peter was in the wrong place to enjoy the blessing of the Lord. In the midst of the enemies of Christ is a poor place for a weak saint. Then Peter "sat." Bad enough to stand there, let alone sit in such a place! When Peter sat down, it looked as though he had no intention to leave that place. He settled down in the midst of circumstances that were contrary to Christian growth.

How would you describe the company you keep? Are they a positive influence on your spiritual life?

Peter wasn't there to defend Christ. He denied Christ by the very position he was in. In verse 69, he was in the palace. In verse 71, he is out on the porch. He went further from Christ with each move he made.

Peter tried to find comfort at the enemies' fires: "Now the servants and the officials had made a charcoal fire, because it was cold. They were standing there warming themselves, and Peter was standing with them, warming himself" (John 18:18). He warmed himself at the world's fire. That kind of comfort never does much good for the body or the soul. No wonder he failed!

Do you frequent places that would be considered "enemies' fires"? What kinds of places should you avoid in order to stay focused on your relationship with Jesus?

Mark's Gospel adds this additional information to the account: "Then he started to curse and swear, 'I don't know this man you're talking about!'" (Mark 14:71). No one would have expected such a remark from Peter. Did he not say, "You are the Messiah, the Son of the living God" (Matt. 16:16)?

Peter failed at what really was his strong point. He was a courageous man. He had shown it in several ways in difficult places. When all had forsaken Christ, Peter stood with drawn sword to defend Him. His outspoken, courageous heart was his strong point, but on this occasion it became his weak point. Here is a place where every Christian must be careful. We are all like Peter.

Peter lied deliberately, and all in the presence of Christ's enemies. It is so easy to lie. We can use language that will shade the truth, so that it will have another meaning. Peter was not careful with the use of his tongue. All of this came from a heart that was defeated. Something was wrong on the inside. Nothing is opened by mistake more than our mouths. Let us beware, let us be wise, and let us be careful about the use of our tongue.

Read John 21:15-17.

What's in a name? A lot, actually. Especially if your name was once Simon, but Jesus changed it to Peter. On the shore of the lake on this particular morning, Jesus no longer called him Peter, but instead reverted to calling the apostle by his former name.

The Lord used the name Peter had in his unregenerate days, before he met the Savior: Simon, son of John. On the night of the betrayal, Peter had used the lies and even the coarse language of his old nature. So Jesus called him by his old name, Simon.

That stabbed Peter's conscience. When Peter first met the Lord, Jesus had said to him: "You are Simon, son of John. You will be called Cephas (which is translated 'Peter')" (John 1:42). When Peter made his great confession, the Lord reconfirmed that: "Blessed are you, Simon son of Jonah, . . . And I also say to you that you are Peter" (Matt. 16:17-18). But now the Lord went back to the old name and left it at that. It is no part of healing a guilty conscience to minimize the seriousness of the offense, nor to conceal the source in the old evil nature from whence it came.

When have you been reminded of a past failure? What was the trigger?

"Do you love me more than these?" The Lord's word was *agapao,* the word for the highest kind of love, the word used for God's love, love that is lofty, spiritual, pure. It is not certain what Jesus meant by "more than these." Did Peter love Jesus more than the fish? After all, he had taken the initiative, he had influenced the others into going back into the fishing business. If he wanted to settle for fish, well, there were plenty of them. Peter could go and sell them and get a good start back in business.

More likely, "more than these" refers to the disciples. Peter had boasted, "'Even if everyone falls away because of you, I will never fall away.' . . . 'Even if I have to die with you,' Peter told him, 'I will never deny you'" (Matt. 26:33,35). He said this in the face of the Lord's prophecy that he would deny Him three times (v. 34). "Do you love me more than these other disciples, Peter?" Was that what the Lord meant? In either case, the Lord probed Peter's conscience.

Peter's answer was prompt, but marked by caution: "Yes, Lord, . . . you know that I love you." Peter used the word *phileo,* meaning brotherly love. "You know, Lord," Peter said, "I have deep affection for you."

"Feed my lambs." The word for "lambs" is *arnion*. It occurs only here and in the Book of Revelation, where it is used of Christ twenty eight times. The other word for "lamb" is used solely of Christ (see 1:29, 36; Acts 8:32; 1 Peter 1:19). The Lord accepted Peter's genuine profession of love and directed him once and for all away from the secular to the spiritual, from the fishing business to the work of a shepherd of God's lambs.

And feed God's lambs Peter did. When we see him again in the Book of Acts, Peter preached his heart out, boldly proclaiming Jesus (Acts 2:14-41). From then on, Peter would no longer be called Simon. Instead, he would be known as Peter, the rock. He remained a committed, bold follower of Christ until his own death and martyrdom.

Are you struggling with a present-day failure that causes you to believe you are unlovable or unusable by God? What is it?

Peter failed the Lord three times, yet Jesus had no words of condemnation for him, only words of restoration. There is no reason you should believe that Jesus won't forgive you and place you back into His service. What He did for Peter, He will do for you.

Read John 21:18-23.

The significance of these verses for the early church is marked by the fact that these words of Jesus are introduced by the well-known "I tell you the truth" expression found repeatedly in the rest of the Gospel.

In this passage, Jesus informs Peter that he must suffer martyrdom as an aspect of his discipleship. That meant that he was obliged to "follow" Jesus, even to the point of crucifixion. In this way he would also glorify God as a faithful disciple who was willing to follow his master to death. Faithful to his personality, Peter was concerned about someone else's life and needed to hear again the emphatic words of Jesus: "Follow me!"

Why do you think Peter asked about John's future?

What is the crucial issue revealed in Jesus' response to Peter?

Like Peter, we tend to focus on comparisons. That is usually the way we try to understand whether we are okay. But that is not the way it works with God. God is concerned about us personally. Of course, God is concerned about our community, our brothers and sisters, our friends, the world. But these can stand in the way of our confronting our own individual responsibilities before God. Our concern for others can actually sidetrack us from facing God's personal demands on us. That was the problem with Peter in this verse, and Jesus was prepared to confront him with this sidetracking of his personal calling.

Why do we sometimes compare our tasks for Christ with the work of others?

What effect does focusing on someone else's role and achievements have? What should be our focus and point of comparison instead?

Peter and John went back a long way with Jesus. Was Peter uneasy about John's future? Would John suffer crucifixion also? Or was Peter just curious about what Jesus would want from John? Perhaps Peter really wondered what the Lord wanted to do in the other disciples' lives. In any case, Jesus declined to give Peter the kind of answer he was seeking. The purpose of Jesus' reply was to cause Peter to focus on his main task of following Jesus. Following Christ and helping His people require focus and a refusal to compare our circumstances with others' circumstances.

TIPS FOR LEADING A SMALL GROUP

Follow these guidelines to prepare for each group session.

PRAYERFULLY PREPARE

Review

Review the weekly material and group questions ahead of time.

Pray

Be intentional about praying for each person in the group. Ask the Holy Spirit to work through you and the group discussion as you point to Jesus each week through God's Word.

MINIMIZE DISTRACTIONS

Create a comfortable environment. If group members are uncomfortable, they'll be distracted and therefore not engaged in the group experience. Plan ahead by considering these details:

Seating

Temperature

Lighting

Food or Drink

Surrounding Noise

General Cleanliness

At best, thoughtfulness and hospitality show guests and group members they're welcome and valued in whatever environment you choose to gather. At worst, people may never notice your effort, but they're also not distracted. Do everything in your ability to help people focus on what's most important: connecting with God, with the Bible, and with one another.

INCLUDE OTHERS

Your goal is to foster a community in which people are welcome just as they are but encouraged to grow spiritually. Always be aware of opportunities to include any people who visit the group and to invite new people to join your group. An inexpensive way to make first-time guests feel welcome or to invite someone to get involved is to give them their own copies of this Bible study book.

ENCOURAGE DISCUSSION

A good small-group experience has the following characteristics.

Everyone Participates

Encourage everyone to ask questions, share responses, or read aloud.

No One Dominates—Not Even the Leader

Be sure that your time speaking as a leader takes up less than half of your time together as a group. Politely guide discussion if anyone dominates.

Nobody Is Rushed Through Questions

Don't feel that a moment of silence is a bad thing. People often need time to think about their responses to questions they've just heard or to gain courage to share what God is stirring in their hearts.

Input Is Affirmed and Followed Up

Make sure you point out something true or helpful in a response. Don't just move on. Build community with follow-up questions, asking how other people have experienced similar things or how a truth has shaped their understanding of God and the Scripture you're studying. People are less likely to speak up if they fear that you don't actually want to hear their answers or that you're looking for only a certain answer.

God and His Word Are Central

Opinions and experiences can be helpful, but God has given us the truth. Trust God's Word to be the authority and God's Spirit to work in people's lives. You can't change anyone, but God can. Continually point people to the Word and to active steps of faith.

HOW TO USE THE LEADER GUIDE

PREPARE TO LEAD

Each session of the Leader Guide is designed to be torn out so you, the leader, can have this front-and-back page with you as you lead your group through the session. Watch the session teaching video and read through the session content with the Leader Guide tear-out in hand and notice how it supplements each section of the study.

FOCUS ATTENTION

These questions are provided to help get the discussion started. They are generally more introductory and topical in nature.

EXPLORE THE TEXT

Questions in this section have some sample answers or discussion prompts provided in the Leader Guide, if needed, to help you jump-start or steer the conversation.

APPLY THE TEXT

This section contains questions that allow group members an opportunity to apply the content they have been discussing together.

BIOGRAPHY AND FURTHER INSIGHT MOMENT

These sections aren't covered in the leader guide and may be used during the group session or by group members as a part of the personal study time during the week. If you choose to use them during your group session, make sure you are familiar with the content and how you intend to use it before your group meets.

Conclude each group session with a prayer.

SESSION 1 | LEADER GUIDE

FOCUS ATTENTION

When was the last time you got so excited about something that you couldn't wait to tell others? What was it, and how did you go about sharing your news?

- Why do Christians get so excited about many things and have no hesitation sharing them with others, but when it comes to sharing the gospel, they grow silent and refuse to speak about the greatest news the world has ever heard?

EXPLORE THE TEXT

Ask a volunteer to read John 1:43-46.

When you look at Philip's story here, what example is there for us to follow?

- Philip immediately followed Jesus when he received the invitation from the Savior. We can do the same. Philip was a new disciple and had an incomplete understanding about who Jesus was and what His mission was, but he didn't let that keep him from inviting others to come to Jesus.

Ask a volunteer to read John 6:1-7.

In another story about Philip's journey with Jesus, the Lord tested him when a crisis arose. How would you describe Philip in this encounter with Jesus?

- Philip was one of Jesus' twelve apostles (see Luke 6:14), but he was still growing in his understanding of who Jesus was. The Lord tested him to see if he had grown in his faith as it related to Christ and His personhood.

- Philip's response was very literal. He quickly realized that almost a year's wages would not be enough to feed the giant crowd. Philip didn't respond in such a way that would indicate he expected Jesus to perform a miracle. He was thinking only about how he and his fellow apostles could solve the dilemma.

Ask a volunteer to read John 12:20-32.

What is significant about Philip, the Greeks who approached Jesus, and the timing of Jesus' reply to the request for an audience with Him?

- The Greeks approached Philip with a request to have an audience with Jesus; they had questions, and they felt comfortable approaching this Jewish rabbi.

- In Jesus' reply (vv. 23-27), we see the reality that His death was going to be for all the people of the world, not just the Jews alone. Jesus' death on the cross was about to pave the way for people of every tribe and tongue to approach God through Jesus. The gospel was not going to be exclusively for the Jews, but for all who earnestly seek Jesus.

Ask a volunteer to read John 14:8-14.

How would you describe Jesus' response to Philip's request to show him and his fellow apostles the Father?

- Jesus almost sounded disappointed in Philip's request. Jesus used the request of Philip to again emphasize His unity with God the Father; seeing Jesus meant they had already seen their heavenly Father.

Ask a volunteer to read Acts 8:4-8,26-40.

What can we know about Philip in this post-resurrection account of his ministry as an apostle? How is he different than he was in the previous passages?

- Philip ministered in Samaria, a region full of people the Jews considered to be "half-breeds" (Jews who had intermarried with people from pagan nations), and to be in proximity to them made a Jew ceremonially unclean. Philip sought them out, as Jesus once did, in order to preach the gospel to them.

- Philip's ministry was effective. Scripture says that he performed many miracles, cast out demons, and healed the crippled among them. Because many accepted Christ as their Savior, there was great joy in the city where he ministered.

- Philip obeyed the angel of the Lord who told him to head south toward Gaza. When the Spirit instructed Philip to get close to an Egyptian official's chariot, he did so immediately. Philip heard the official reading from the Book of Isaiah, and he offered to explain the Scripture to him.

APPLY THE TEXT

With which part of Philip's life can you most easily identify? His early days or his time after Jesus' resurrection? Explain.

For a time, Philip had misunderstandings about who Jesus was. Is there any aspect of Jesus' life and ministry that is confusing to you?

Who do you know who needs to hear the good news about Jesus and the reality that they can be forgiven of their sin and have a new life in Christ? What would it take for you to have the boldness of Philip and share the good news with them this week?

SESSION 2 | LEADER GUIDE

Focus Attention

When you think about change, who do you know who has changed in positive ways over the time you've known him or her? What factors cause people to take action and change some aspect of themselves or their lives?

- People often take action to change when they seek to improve themselves physically, spiritually, or emotionally. Others seek change when the pain of staying as they are is greater than the pain of change.

Explore The Text

Ask a volunteer to read John 3:1-3.

What do we learn about Nicodemus in these verses? What was missing in his life, according to Jesus (v. 3)?

- Nicodemus was a Pharisee and someone with authority and respect since he was a member of the Jewish ruling council.

- Nicodemus came to Jesus at night to perhaps hide his curiosity and connection with Jesus, not wanting to offend members of his party. Nicodemus needed a new understanding about how people enter the kingdom of heaven.

Ask a volunteer to read John 3:4-8.

What did Jesus want Nicodemus to know by His statement in verse 8? How does this apply to us?

- The wind's origin is not seen, but its effects are. It is the same with people born of the Spirit. You can't observe the Holy Spirit with your eyes, but you can observe His work in the hearts and lives of people who are born again. This applies to us today just as it did to the people of Nicodemus' day.

Ask a volunteer to read John 3:9-13.

What did Nicodemus mean by his question in verse 9? What can we learn from Jesus' response to him?

- Nicodemus heard Jesus' words about being born again being a requirement for entering heaven. He may have asked his question from a point of complete misunderstanding or to say, "You're not telling me the truth! I don't believe it!"

- Jesus declares the accuracy of His teaching by saying "I tell you the truth" at the beginning of verse 11, and asserts that He is speaking about things of which He has direct knowledge. Not to believe Him would be foolish.

Ask a volunteer to read John 3:14-16.

What does the reference to Moses and the snake being lifted up have to do with John 3:16?

- The reference to Moses lifting up the snake in the desert recalls an event during which poisonous snakes bit Israelites who had sinned against Moses. A bronze snake was made and attached to a pole, and when people were bitten, they could look at the snake on the pole in faith, and would not die from their wounds.

- John 3:16 describes God's ultimate act of love towards mankind—the sacrificial death of His Son on a cross for the forgiveness of our sins.

Ask a volunteer to read John 3:17-18.

Why might some people struggle with the teachings in these verses?

- Some people will struggle to accept these words because they believe "God is love" and will not condemn anyone to hell. Others might struggle because this exclusivity about Jesus being the only way makes Christianity appear to have an exclusive truth that is offensive to people of different religious backgrounds.

Ask a volunteer to read John 3:19-21.

In light of Jesus' earlier conversation with Nicodemus, why do you believe Jesus ended His interaction with "Israel's teacher" in this way?

- Because Nicodemus had difficulty accepting Jesus' teaching, and may have openly challenged the truthfulness of Jesus' testimony, Jesus wraps up their conversation by focusing on the fact that truth and light (Jesus and the gospel) have come into the world, but men have rejected both the truth and the testimony of heaven.

APPLY THE TEXT

Why do people find it difficult to accept Jesus' testimony about how one comes into His eternal family?

How can we help others accept Jesus' offer of forgiveness?

How does the growing idea that truth is relative and even geographical make it harder for people to accept God's Word and salvation through Christ?

SESSION 3 | LEADER GUIDE

FOCUS ATTENTION

How has our ability to converse with one another been positively or negatively impacted by the rise of social media and electronic methods of communication?

EXPLORE THE TEXT

Ask a volunteer to read John 4:1-3.

Why would Jesus and His disciples leave Judea, where they were beginning to experience success in ministry?

- Success aroused the attention of the religious leaders, the Pharisees. To avoid confrontation with these leaders, Jesus and His disciples journeyed north from Judea through Samaria with an ultimate destination of Galilee.

- Jesus' withdrawal was not a sign of defeat, but a tactical move to ensure that the Pharisees didn't interfere in His mission and work too prematurely. At the right time, Jesus would confront them, but for now, He avoided handing them the ability to circumvent His ministry and force a confrontation with Him.

Ask a volunteer to read John 4:4-9.

Why do you think Jesus traveled through Samaria? What was strange about this?

- Jesus and His disciples left Jerusalem for Galilee, traveling by way of Samaria. Jews in those days tried to avoid the Samaritan route, because they considered the people in the region to be ceremonially unclean.

- Traveling through Samaria was the fastest route to get to Galilee. Jesus could have traveled around Samaria, but it would have cost a lot of time, and He was about to demonstrate to His disciples that the good news of the kingdom of God was for all people, not only the Jews. He was on the verge of showing the world that the gospel is for all people.

Ask a volunteer to read John 4:10-12.

In what ways did the woman misunderstand Jesus in His conversation with her?

- The Samaritan woman misunderstood who she was talking to. Jesus appeared to be nothing more than a weary, parched traveler—and a Jew—who was tired. She didn't immediately recognize Him as the promised Messiah.

- The Samaritan woman misunderstood her opportunity—to ask the Savior for forgiveness of her sins that would lead to eternal life ("living water"). She did not equate "living water" with eternal life yet.

Ask a volunteer to read John 4:13-19.

How did Jesus begin to reveal His true self to the Samaritan woman?

- Jesus told the woman to go and call her husband, and then come back. The woman told Jesus she had no husband, which was technically correct.

- Jesus didn't condemn the Samaritan woman, but revealed to her that He knew she had been married five times, and the man she lived with now was not her husband officially. This was something no one could know, except a man of God with special insight. Hence, she called Jesus a prophet and began to suspect there was more to Him than met the eye.

Ask a volunteer to read John 4:25-26 and John 4:27-30,39-42.

How did the Samaritan woman respond once Jesus revealed His true identity? What important things followed this revelation?

- The Samaritan woman, who had avoided people at midday, immediately went into her town and began telling people about her encounter with Jesus. She invited them to come back with her to see whether or not He was truly the promised Messiah.

- Because of her simple testimony that Jesus knew all about her past and told her everything she'd ever done, many Samaritans believed in Him.

- The Samaritan townspeople initially believed because of the woman's testimony, but after spending two days with Jesus themselves, and listening to His testimony, many more became believers.

APPLY THE TEXT

Do you feel as if there are reasons you aren't good enough for Jesus? How does this story speak against this feeling?

How can you use your testimony and salvation story to share the message of Christ?

In what people or things are you most tempted to look for fulfillment instead of looking to Christ? How can we hold one another accountable to look only to Christ this week?

SESSION 4 | LEADER GUIDE

FOCUS ATTENTION

How would you describe your personality? Who do you take after more—your father or mother? How are you similar to or different from your siblings?

EXPLORE THE TEXT

Ask a volunteer to read Luke 10:38-42.

What was Jesus trying to help Martha understand by his statements in verses 41-42? What lessons can we learn from this encounter?

- Jesus tried to help Martha realize that although the preparation for the meal and the evening itself was filled with important tasks, Mary had chosen what was better—spending time with Him.

- Life can be full of distractions—even good things—that keep our focus off Jesus. We should make certain we aren't so overly busy and worried with the cares of life that we miss out on spending time with Jesus in prayer, meditation on His Word, and fellowship with His people.

Martha's relationships with Jesus and her sister were strained because of her distractions and cares about creating the "perfect" evening. What is the warning for us?

- People may not always do what we expect they should do. In those cases, we shouldn't allow our frustrations to rise up and cause damage to our relationship with them.

Ask a volunteer to read John 11:1-6,11-14.

What additional information do you get about Mary, Martha, and Lazarus from these verses?

- The women's brother, Lazarus, had become sick.

- Mary had earlier poured oil on Jesus' feet as a sign of her devotion to Him.

- Jesus loved Lazarus, and the two sisters had no hesitation calling for Jesus to return to their home to heal him.

- Jesus told His disciples that He was going to journey to Bethany and "wake him up."

How do you explain the apparent discrepancy in Jesus' words about Lazarus in verses 4 and 11-14?

- Jesus stated in verse 4 that Lazarus' disease would not end in his death; just a short time later, though, Jesus told the disciples plainly that "Lazarus is dead" (v. 14). Jesus had power over death, and no matter if Lazarus died, Jesus could raise him to life. The end result would be the same: Lazarus would live.

Ask a volunteer to read John 11:17-27.

How was Martha's response to Jesus' arrival and her stated beliefs both on target and slightly off target?

- Martha was on-target in her assessment of who Jesus was—she properly identified Him as the promised Messiah (v. 27). She also believed in the resurrection of the dead (v. 24).

- Martha was slightly off-target because even though she anticipated a resurrection at the last day, she didn't yet connect the fact that Jesus, the Messiah, could provide a resurrection for her brother well in advance of the last day.

Ask a volunteer to read John 11:38-44.

Why was Jesus so moved by the death of Lazarus?

- Lazarus was a friend whom Jesus loved. But standing at his tomb, the effects of sin were on full display. Standing in front of Lazarus' tomb, the reality of sin's power could be seen because of Lazarus' dead body and the sadness and grief that death had caused the sisters and their friends.

- Jesus may have been moved, too, because He would soon head to Jerusalem and His death on the cross to undo sin's effect on the human race.

APPLY THE TEXT

What different forms of busyness take over in your life?

What kinds of things in your life—even seemingly "spiritual" things—might distract you from choosing intimacy with Jesus over activity?

What situation are you facing today that seems insurmountable? Based on Jesus' power over death and the grave, is there any reason that Jesus couldn't provide deliverance for you?

SESSION 5 | LEADER GUIDE

FOCUS ATTENTION

When have you experienced a period of doubt with regard to your faith? What were the circumstances?

EXPLORE THE TEXT

Ask a volunteer to read John 20:19.

Based on verse 19 alone, what can we surmise about the disciples?

- The Bible says the disciples were meeting in the evening, which may have been done to hide their identities as they traveled to the place of meeting.

- The doors to the place they met were locked, and the Bible clearly says it was because they were afraid of the Jews—those religious leaders had just killed Jesus, and the disciples may have reasoned that Jesus' followers might be next.

- In a time of loss and confusion, the disciples banded together to comfort one another and encourage the entire group, even though they had lost their leader, Jesus.

Ask a volunteer to read John 20:20-23.

According to Luke 24:37, the disciples believed they were seeing a ghost. How did Jesus' response to their fears disprove this idea?

- Jesus conclusively proved that he was not a ghost without a body, but was indeed a person with a real body, a body that still bore the scars from the crucifixion He had endured just days ago.

What things do you notice about Jesus' commission of His disciples in verses 21-22?

- Jesus reminded the disciples that He had been sent into the world "to seek and to save the lost." Similarly, He was imparting that same mission to the disciples. God had sent the Son into the world; now the Son sent the disciples into that same world.

- The disciples needed the power and presence of the Holy Spirit to accomplish their mission. Jesus breathed on them as a sign of Him giving the Holy Spirit to them. He could simply have spoken this, but He did something memorable so they could remember always that He had poured out the Spirit on them.

- All three members of the Godhead are present at this commissioning service. God has sent Christ into the world, and Jesus fulfilled His Father's will. Now the Holy Spirit was given to the disciples. In giving us this information, we can see that the Trinity (Father, Son, Holy Spirit) are intimately and collectively involved in providing salvation for mankind through Christ's atoning death.

Ask a volunteer to read John 20:24-31.

Thomas was absent from the gathering where Jesus revealed Himself to the disciples. Why might he have been so adamant about seeing Jesus for himself?

- Thomas has been called "Doubting Thomas" by Christians because of his response to his fellow disciples. Thomas may not have believed the testimony of his fellow disciples because of what he perceived as the finality of death. He may also have felt the disciples were playing a joke on him. Or even still, Thomas may have just been hard-headed and skeptical by nature, thinking that the disciples saw a ghost and simply thought they'd seen a real body.

How does Thomas's response in verse 25, and Jesus' statement that follows, apply to us today?

- Thomas finally believed and affirmed that Jesus was Lord. Thomas acknowledged that Jesus was indeed alive.

- Jesus said that Thomas believed because he had seen, but others (you and I) would be blessed with eternal life because we would one day believe that Jesus is alive and that He is God, even though we didn't have the advantage of seeing Him or being able to place our hands and fingers into His wounds. We would be blessed because we would believe by faith that Jesus is the promised Messiah.

APPLY THE TEXT

Where could you use Jesus' peace right now?

What doubts or questions about God are you struggling with today?

Have you received the gift of the Holy Spirit? How has He changed you?

SESSION 6 | LEADER GUIDE

FOCUS ATTENTION

What is something you have restored? How did you feel once the job was complete?

- People may have restored a car, a piece of furniture, or something much larger like a home. When a restoration job is complete, there is a sense of satisfaction and accomplishment.

- People sometimes find themselves in need of restoration to God because they have allowed sin to ruin the fellowship they once had with Him. Such was the case with the apostle Peter.

EXPLORE THE TEXT

Ask a volunteer to read John 18:15-18.

How would you describe Peter in these verses?

- Peter appeared to want to blend in and be unrecognizable. When asked by a slave girl if he was one of Jesus' disciples, he quickly replied that he was not. When Peter was brought into the home of the high priest, he blended in with the people in the courtyard by standing by the fire, because to separate himself on a cold night would have drawn much attention.

Ask a volunteer to read John 18:25-27.

What do you notice about Peter's second and third denials of Christ in these verses?

- Peter had no hesitation denying his relationship to Jesus. The people who asked the second time were servants (see Matthew 26:71 and Luke 22:58).

- Peter's third denial was made to a relative of the man whose ear Peter cut off in the garden where Jesus had been praying. Because a charcoal fire glows, but has no flame, the light was probably poor and dim, and Peter continued to go unnoticed as a disciple of Jesus.

- As soon as Peter fulfilled Jesus' prophecy about denying Him three times, the rooster crowed. This verified that Jesus had indeed been correct that Peter would deny Him and fail Him three times that night.

Ask a volunteer to read John 21:1-7.

How did John recognize the Lord before announcing it to the rest of the disciples in the boat?

- John may have recognized Jesus' words and the situation (the boat, the fish) as very similar to Jesus' calling of the first disciples in Galilee. Something about the entire situation reminded John of the day that Jesus called His first disciples.

Why did Peter immediately jump into the water and swim to shore?

- Peter loved Jesus and was excited to be able to see Him and speak with Him again. Perhaps Peter wanted to show Jesus his enthusiasm and in some way make amends for failing Him three times the night before His crucifixion.

Ask a volunteer to read John 21:15-22.

What is the significance of Jesus' three questions to Peter?

- Peter had been asked three questions about his relationship to Jesus the night before Jesus' crucifixion. He failed all three times to testify correctly that he was indeed one of Jesus' disciples. Jesus' three questions may have been intended to remind Peter that he had failed miserably at the earlier set of questions. Now he had a chance to get all three questions right.

Why did Peter ask a question about the fate of John?

- Perhaps Peter sensed what Jesus was telling him about his future death and glorification of God through it, and Peter was curious about John's fate as well.

- Jesus quickly rebuked Peter and refused to answer his question asking, "What is that to you?" (v. 22) Jesus told Peter that the only thing he needed to concern himself with was his obedience to Jesus. The obedience of others was not Peter's concern—he needed to focus on his relationship to Christ.

APPLY THE TEXT

In what ways do you find yourself in need of restoration to God?

Where do you find encouragement in this story of Peter, his denial, and his restoration into ministry?

Peter told the Lord that he loved Him (three times). What might someone observe in your daily life that shows how much you love the Lord?

Then he said to Thomas,
"Put your finger here
and look at my hands.
Reach out your hand
and put it into my side.
Don't be faithless,
but believe."

JOHN 20:27

Whether you're a new Christian or you have believed in Jesus for several years, the people of the Bible have so much wisdom to offer. For that reason, we have created additional resources for churches that want to maximize the reach and impact of the *Characters* studies.

Complete Series Leader Pack

Want to take your group through the whole *Explore the Bible: Characters* series? You'll want a *Complete Series Leader Pack*. This *Pack* includes *Leader Kits* from Volume 1 - Volume 7. It allows you to take your group from The Patriarchs all the way to The Early Church Leaders.

$179.99

Video Bundle for Groups

All video sessions are available to purchase as a downloadable bundle.

$60.00

eBooks

A digital version of the *Bible Study Book* is also available for those who prefer studying with a phone or tablet. Some churches also find eBooks easier to distribute to study participants.

Starter Packs

You can save money and time by purchasing starter packs for your group or church. Every *Church Starter Pack* includes a digital *Church Launch Kit* and access to a digital version of the *Leader Kit* videos.

$99.99 | **Single Group Starter Pack**
(10 *Bible Study Books*, 1 *Leader Kit*)

$449.99 | **Small Church Starter Pack**
(50 *Bible Study Books*, 5 *Leader Kit* DVDs, and access to video downloads)

$799.99 | **Medium Church Starter Pack**
(100 *Bible Study Books*, 10 *Leader Kit* DVDs, and access to video downloads)

$3495.99 | **Large Church Starter Pack**
(500 *Bible Study Books*, 50 *Leader Kit* DVDs, and access to video downloads)

LifeWay.com/characters
Order online or call 800.458.2772.

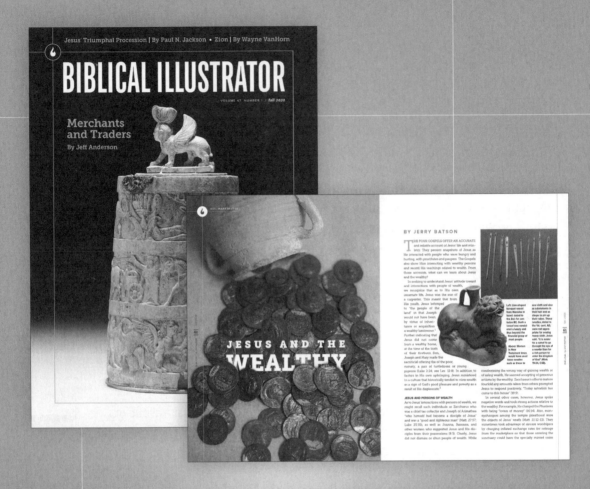

WANT TO KNOW EVEN MORE ABOUT BIBLICAL CHARACTERS?

The *Explore the Bible: Characters* series features information from the pages of *Biblical Illustrator*. And there are more insights on the way. Every quarter, you'll find remarkable content that will greatly enhance your study of the Bible:

- Fascinating photographs, illustrations, maps, and archaeological finds
- Informative articles on biblical lands, people, history, and customs
- Insights about how people lived, learned, and worshiped in biblical times

Order at lifeway.com/biblicalillustrator or call 800.458.2772.

Continue Your
Exploration

---------------------------------- VOLUME 7 ----------------------------------

THE EARLY CHURCH LEADERS

Studying the characters of the Bible helps us understand how God works in the world, loves His people, and moves through His people to accomplish His plans. The next and final volume of *Explore the Bible: Characters* focuses on Stephen, Paul, Barnabas, James, Priscilla & Aquila, and Timothy. These early church leaders may have the most to teach us about living in the modern church era.

Bible Study Book 005823509 **$9.99**
Leader Kit 005823543 **$29.99**

EXPLORE YOUR OPTIONS

EXPLORE THE BIBLE

EXPLORE THE BIBLE

If you want to understand the Bible in its historical, cultural, and biblical context, few resources offer the thoroughness of the Explore the Bible ongoing quarterly curriculum. Over the course of nine years, you can study the whole truth, book by book, in a way that's practical, sustainable, and age appropriate for your entire church.

6- TO 8-WEEK STUDIES

If you're looking for short-term resources that are more small-group friendly, visit the LifeWay website to see Bible studies from a variety of noteworthy authors, including Ravi Zacharias, J.D. Greear, Matt Chandler, David Platt, Tony Evans, and many more.

Prices and availability subject to change without notice.